TIGER WOODS

TIGER WOODS

A Biography

Lawrence J. Londino

GREENWOOD BIOGRAPHIES

GREENWOOD PRESS
WESTPORT, CONNECTICUT · LONDON

Library of Congress Cataloging-in-Publication Data

Londino, Lawrence J.
    Tiger Woods : a biography / Lawrence J. Londino.
      p. cm. — (Greenwood biographies, ISSN 1540–4900)
    Includes bibliographical references and index.
    ISBN 0–313–33121–9
    1. Woods, Tiger. 2. Golfers—United States—Biography. I. Title. II. Series.
GV964.W66L66   2005
796.352'092—dc22   2005020070

British Library Cataloguing in Publication Data is available.

This book is included in the *African American Experience* database from Greenwood
Electronic Media. For more information, visit www.africanamericanexperience.com.

Library of Congress Catalog Card Number: 2005020070
ISBN: 0–313–33121–9
ISSN: 1540–4900

First published in 2006

Greenwood Press, 88 Post Road West, Westport, CT 06881
An imprint of Greenwood Publishing Group, Inc.
www.greenwood.com

Printed in the United States of America

The paper used in this book complies with the
Permanent Paper Standard issued by the National
Information Standards Organization (Z39.48–1984).

10 9 8 7 6 5 4 3 2 1

CONTENTS

Photo essay follows page 38

ACKNOWLEDGMENTS

I would like to make acknowledgments for acts, without which this book would probably have remained an ambition: my administrative assistant for the Department of Broadcasting at Montclair State University, Stephanie Wood, who provided invaluable editorial support, and my sons Paul, James, and Jonathan, my sister Elaine and dear mother, whose Christmas gift of an exceedingly comfortable padded desk chair for my basement office removed my final excuse for not getting started.

SERIES FOREWORD

In response to high school and public library needs, Greenwood developed this distinguished series of full-length biographies specifically for student use. Prepared by field experts and professionals, these engaging biographies are tailored for high school students who need challenging yet accessible biographies. Ideal for secondary school assignments, the length, format and subject areas are designed to meet educators' requirements and students' interests.

Greenwood offers an extensive selection of biographies spanning all curriculum related subject areas including social studies, the sciences, literature and the arts, history and politics, as well as popular culture, covering public figures and famous personalities from all time periods and backgrounds, both historic and contemporary, who have made an impact on American and/or world culture. Greenwood biographies were chosen based on comprehensive feedback from librarians and educators. Consideration was given to both curriculum relevance and inherent interest. The result is an intriguing mix of the well known and the unexpected, the saints and sinners from long-ago history and contemporary pop culture. Readers will find a wide array of subject choices from fascinating crime figures like Al Capone to inspiring pioneers like Margaret Mead, from the greatest minds of our time like Stephen Hawking to the most amazing success stories of our day like J.K. Rowling.

While the emphasis is on fact, not glorification, the books are meant to be fun to read. Each volume provides in-depth information about the subject's life from birth through childhood, the teen years, and adulthood. A thorough account relates family background and education, traces personal and professional influences, and explores struggles, accomplishments, and contributions. A timeline highlights the most significant life events against a historical perspective. Bibliographies supplement the reference value of each volume.

INTRODUCTION

I first heard of Tiger Woods in 1985 while doing research for a television documentary about the history of African Americans in golf. Whenever one of my colleagues at New York University asked me what I was working on, the standard chiding response was "That will be a pretty short documentary." Eventually I discovered evidence of African Americans playing the game of golf all the way back to colonial days. So while Tiger Woods is not the first person of color to master the game of golf, nobody, of any color, has garnered as much attention. An informal internet search for Tiger Woods yields some 1,780,000 websites—Arnold Palmer warrants 576,000. But still, a central question has to be posed and answered: Why write a biography of a person who is, as of this publication, 29 years old, and still very much alive?

Tiger Woods was a golf prodigy. By the age of three, he had already mastered the rudimentary skills of the game, was regularly covered by local and national media, and had appeared on the Mike Douglas show, where he demonstrated his remarkable skills. But unlike many child prodigies, he delivered on his early promise, winning an unprecedented three consecutive United States Golf Association Junior Championships, and eventually duplicating the feat at the USGA Amateur Championship, the most prestigious amateur title in golf. He won the NCAA Championship (individual) as a student athlete at Stanford University.

Woods made the transition to professional golf seamlessly. To date, he has won over 40 professional golf tournaments, including ten major championships, which are universally accepted as the most coveted titles. His mixed African American/Thai/Chinese/Native American/Caucasian racial heritage further underscored his achievements in a historically segregated sport. He grew up in a very normal middle-class suburban Northern California neighborhood, attended public schools and, while competing in professional tournaments as a teenager, was a regular member of his high school golf team. These reasons alone would justify this book. However, the phenomenon of Tiger Woods goes beyond his extremely high profile in the world of golf and sports.

After signing his first contract with the Nike Company he began to apply his superstar celebrity status and fortune to a variety of philanthropic activities which, because of his high profile, could eventually have significant impact on American and world culture. And he's accomplished all this as a racially mixed man in a predominately white society.

There is a tendency to be overwhelmed by these vaguely messianic prophecies when talking about Tiger Woods. It's hard not to. This book will endeavor to examine this short but extremely accomplished life. The role of parents is always an important element of any biography. But when an individual is so young, his parents will necessarily be major elements in the story. His father, Earl Woods, had the greatest influence on the evolution of Tiger Woods. This is also the story of how Earl grew up in the middle of the United States in the time before Civil Rights and how that shaped his life. And of his mother, Kultida, who was born in Thailand and came to this country as the wife of a black man.

A significant part of this story has to do with the game of golf. The unique characteristics of this truly international game, the intense individual adherence to the rules and its generally elite origins all played a role in the evolution of Tiger Woods.

As with any pioneer, there are always others who made sacrifices and endured hardship to make it possible for followers to succeed. So this book will introduce some of these early African American golfers who were not allowed to join the Professional Golfers Association until 1961, and explore how their achievements paved the way for Tiger Woods.

This is not, strictly speaking, a sports biography. It's the story of a sports prodigy who accomplished unimagined records in the sport of golf in a very short time span. But at its heart it's a story about a middle-class family struggling to assimilate into a majority culture and along the way how it produced arguably the greatest golfer of all times.

TIMELINE: EVENTS IN THE LIFE OF TIGER WOODS

Born—December 30, 1975

1978–1981   Appeared on *CBS News* and *Mike Douglas Show* putting with Bob Hope

Shot 48 for nine holes at Navy Golf Club in Cypress, Calif.

Appeared on "That's Incredible" television program

1982–1989   Appeared on "Today Show," "Good Morning America," ESPN, CBS, NBC and ABC

Won the Optimist International Junior World at ages 8, 9, 12 and 13

Finished Second place at the Insurance Youth Golf Classic (Big "I") National at age 13

1990   Won the Optimist International Junior World

The youngest winner of the Insurance Youth Golf Classic (Big "I") National

1991   American Junior Golf Association Player of the Year

Golf Digest Junior Player of the Year

Southern California Player of the Year

Titleist-Golfweek National Amateur of the Year

First Team, Rolex Junior All-American

Participated in U.S. Amateur Championship

1992   Played in Nissan Los Angeles Open on PGA Tour and U.S. Open Sectional Qualifier

Top 32, U.S. Amateur Championship

First Team, Rolex Junior All-American

Golf Digest Player of the Year

Southern California Player of the Year
Titleist-Golfweek National Amateur of the Year
Golf World Player of the Year

1993   Winner of the U.S. Junior Amateur Championship
Top 32, U.S. Amateur Championship
First Team, Rolex Junior All-American
Played in three PGA Tour tournaments, the Nissan Los Angeles Open and the Honda Classic and the GTE Byron Nelson Classic
Played in the U.S. Open Sectional Qualifying
Accepted scholarship at Stanford University in November, 1993, to join freshmen class of 1994

1994   Winner of the U.S. Amateur Championship, played at TPC Sawgrass in Ponte Vedra Beach, Fla.
Winner of the Western Amateur Championship
Winner of the Southern California Golf Association Amateur Championship
Winner of the Pacific Northwest Amateur Championship
Member of the United States Team at the World Amateur Team Championships in Versailles, France
Golf World Man of the Year

1995   Winner of the U.S. Amateur Championship, played at Newport Country Club, Newport, R.I.
Tied for 41st in the Masters Tournament, and was the only amateur to make the 36-hole cut
Tied 67th in the British Open at St. Andrews, Scotland
Member, United States Team in Walker Cup Match in Porthcawl, Wales
First Team College All-American
Stanford's Male Freshman of the Year

1996   Named *Sports Illustrated* Sportsman of the Year
PGA Tour Rookie of the Year
Winner of the U.S. Amateur Championship, Pumpkin Ridge Golf Club, Cornelius, Oreg., becoming the only golfer ever to win three consecutive amateur titles
Winner of the NCAA Championship, The Honors Course, Chattanooga, Tenn. with a score of 285
Named the Fred Haskins College Player of the Year
Named unanimous First Team College All-American
Finished tied for 82nd in U.S. Open

Tied British Open 72-hole record for an amateur with total of 281 at Royal Lytham & St. Annes, England

Advanced to No. 33 on the world ranking, the fastest rise into the top 50 in history

1997   Named Associated Press Male Athlete of the Year

Named ESPY Male Athlete of the Year

Leading money winner on PGA Tour, won $2,440,831 worldwide in 25 events

Winner of the Masters Tournament—72-hole record with a total of 270 and set Masters record with 12-stroke victory margin, and became the youngest champion and first major champion of African or Asian heritage

Qualified for United States Team for Ryder Cup Matches

1998   In two years as a professional, ending with NEC World Series of Golf, won $4,561,494 on PGA Tour ($5,300,204 worldwide) with seven victories and 26 top-10 finishes in 47 events (nine victories and 30 top-10 finishes in 55 events worldwide), won $2,927,006 worldwide in 26 events to surpass 1997 earnings of $2,440,832

Qualified for United States Team for Presidents Cup

Held current PGA Tour record for most consecutive events without missing the cut (17). Has missed only one cut in 48 events since joining PGA Tour 1996

1999   Named the Associated Press Male Athlete of the Year for the second time in three years and the seventh man—and the second golfer—to earn the award twice since it was begun in 1931

ESPY Male Athlete of the Year and ESPY Golfer of the Decade

Player of the Year as selected by PGA Tour, PGA of America and Golf Writers Association of America

Leading money winner on PGA Tour with $6,616,585

Mark H. McCormack Award winner as the No. 1 player on the 1999 Official World Golf Ranking.

Qualified for United States Team for Ryder Cup Matches

His eight PGA Tour victories and 11 overall were the most in one year at such a young age since Horton Smith had 8 PGA Tour victories in 1929

Won four consecutive PGA Tour events, the first to do that since Ben Hogan in 1953

2000   *Sports Illustrated* Sportsman of the Year, and became the first person to win the award more than once
The Associated Press Male Athlete of the Year
ESPY Male Athlete of the Year for the third time in four years
Player of the Year as selected by PGA Tour, PGA of America and Golf Writers Association of America
The Sporting News Most Powerful Person in Sports
L'Equipe (France) World Champion of Champions
Reuters Sportsman of the Year
Lowest actual scoring average (68.17), breaking Byron Nelson's record from 1945
Lowest adjusted scoring average (67.79) for Byron Nelson Award (PGA Tour) and Vardon Trophy (PGA of America)
Leading money winner on PGA Tour with $9,188,321 (most ever won in a single year)
Mark H. McCormack Award winner as the No.1 player on the 2000 Official World Golf Ranking
Winner of the U.S. Open Championship, tying Open record with 272 total (65-69-71-67)
Winner of the British Open Championship, setting British Open and Major championship records for the lowest score in relation to par, 19 under par, 269
Winner of the PGA Championship, setting the PGA Championship record for the lowest score in relation to par, 18 under par, 270
Qualified for United States Team for Presidents Cup
Became the first ever to have won the U.S. Open, U.S. Amateur and U.S. Junior Amateur titles
With British Open victory, became the fifth ever and the youngest to complete the career Grand Slam of professional major championships
With PGA Championship victory, became the first since Ben Hogan in 1953 to win three major championships in the same year. Hogan won the Masters, U.S. Open, and British Open

2001   Winner of the Masters Tournament to become the first golfer ever to hold all four professional major championships at the same time

Selected as Player of the Year by PGA Tour, PGA of America and Golf Writers Association of America

Lowest adjusted scoring average (68.81) for Byron Nelson Award and Vardon Trophy

Leading money winner on PGA Tour with $5,687,777

Mark H. McCormack Award winner as the No. 1 player on the 2001 Official World Golf Ranking

2002   Winner of the Masters Tournament

Selected as Player of the Year by PGA Tour, PGA of America and Golf Writers Association of America

Leading money winner on PGA Tour with $6,912,625

Second player to be leading money winner on PGA Tour for four consecutive years

Qualified for United States Team for Ryder Cup Matches

Became the first ever to have won two or more titles each in the U.S. Open, U.S. Amateur, and U.S. Junior Amateur

2003   Selected Player of the Year by PGA Tour, PGA of America and Golf Writers Association of America

Won $6,673,413 on PGA Tour

Mark H. McCormack Award winner as the No. 1 player on the 2003 Official World Golf Ranking

Qualified for United States Team for Presidents Cup

First player to win at least five events on PGA Tour every year for five consecutive years

2004   Qualified for United States Team for Ryder Cup Matches

Career money leader on PGA Tour with $45,142,737

Set record with 334 total weeks as No. 1 on the Official World Golf Ranking, through the list of August 29, 2004 (Previous record was 331 weeks by Greg Norman)

Mark H. McCormack Award winner as the No. 1 player on the 2004 Official World Golf Ranking

Married Elin Nordegren on October 5, 2004

2005   Winner of the Buick Invitational

Winner Doral Open

Winner of the Masters Tournament

Winner of the British Open Championship at St. Andrews Golf Club

Chapter 1

EARLY LIFE

Golf in America has not historically been a sport for the common man. In spite of the fact that golf, as we know it, was first played by Scottish shepherds and soldiers in the thirteenth century, by the time the game made its way to America at the end of the eighteenth century, only people of means played the game. It wasn't until Francis Quimet, a scrappy amateur and former caddy from the other side of the tracks in Brookline, Massachusetts, upset two of England's best professionals in a playoff for the 1913 United States Open that the game began to capture the fancy of the masses. However, golf has always been associated with wealth and privilege.

All the more ironic that, during the writing of this book, the number one ranked golfer in the world is an American of color—in fact, many colors. Eldrick "Tiger" Woods is an amalgam of five different races: African American, Native American, Caucasian, Thai, and Chinese. And it's hard to resist judging his accomplishments against the stereotypical characteristics of these races. In many ways he represents them admirably: determination, physical prowess, mental acuity and spiritual calm. But just as no stereotype holds completely faithful, the same can be said of him. Ultimately, the story of Tiger Woods is not a simple analysis of his genetic makeup.

Tiger was born Eldrick Woods on December 30, 1975. His father, Earl Woods, nicknamed him Tiger in honor of a Vietnamese officer with whom he served in Vietnam. When Tiger was born his father was 44, recently retired from the military, divorced and not particularly anxious to start another family. He already had three children from a previous marriage and had purposely sought to locate somewhere close to these children in Northern California. Tiger's mother, Kultida Punswad, had met Earl while he was serving in Thailand during the Vietnam war in 1967 and had quickly adjusted to life in America. Thai culture doesn't recognize a marriage as fully consummated until there are children and Kultida persisted in her desire to have a child and ultimately persevered.[1]

Even though it was the mid 1970s in one of the most ethnically diverse states in the Union, Earl and his new wife faced instances of discrimination in Southern California. After several incidents where house prices suddenly increased when Earl appeared in person, he was convinced that there was a reluctance to sell to African Americans. The Woods were able to rent his broker's condominium temporarily. There were instances of Kultida being shunned by other wives at the condominium pool. An ugly incident occurred when Earl's eighteen year old son from his first marriage, Earl Jr., who was living with Earl Sr. at the time, was harassed by the local police for trying to park his car in the Woods's garage. Eventually they were able to purchase a house in Cypress, California, where Tiger was raised.

INTRODUCTION TO GOLF

Earl Woods developed an interest in golf while stationed in Fort Hamilton in 1973. Given Earl's innate competitiveness, he wasn't satisfied playing the game simply for exercise and recreation. He approached the game with the same dogged determination that he had demonstrated throughout his life. Since he retired from the Army and was working as a consultant for McDonnell Douglas, he had limited time to actually play or practice golf, so when he did, he wanted to make the most of those opportunities. By the time Tiger was born, Earl had become a single-digit handicap golfer, which meant he was among approximately eight percent of excellent recreational players.[2] He set up a net in his garage and began regularly to go back there after work and pound golf balls to perfect his golf swing. In an effort to relieve his wife from the day-long rigors of watching the baby, he began taking Tiger out to the garage and put him in a baby seat to watch Earl while he practiced. A fairly accomplished athlete in his own right, Earl possessed a decent swing. There were indications even before Tiger was born that this child would have a special affinity for the game. Earl tells of playing in a golf tournament in Lake Shastina in Northern California when his wife, who was pregnant with Tiger, walked along with him on the course. He claims that the "in vitro" Tiger was noticeably agitated in his mother's stomach every place on the golf course except when his mother approached a green. For some unexplained reason he seemed to stop moving when the players were putting.[3]

Earl has described the unusual fascination with the golf swing that his baby son exhibited.[4] He notes that the small child very rarely let his concentration waiver as he watched for hours while his father hit golf balls into a net. Earl was surprised when at the age of nine months, barely able to walk, Tiger picked up a club and swung and hit his first golf ball. By the age of 18 months, Tiger was accompanying his father to the driving range and hitting golf balls.

As a veteran Earl had playing privileges at the Navy course at Los Alamitos where he played regularly.[5] He brought Tiger with him to play on a regulation length golf course at an early age. When eventually Tiger began to play without his father, the authorities at the clubs selectively enforced a rule that young players had to be at least 10 to play without adult supervision—despite the fact that Tiger and his father observed other kids regularly violating this rule. But access to a golf course at this early age undoubtedly precipitated his rapid improvement. By the age of four he managed to shoot 48 for nine holes.[6] He scored his first birdie on a regulation golf course before he was five years old.

There is no evidence that Earl Woods had a master plan for creating a golf superstar before Tiger was born. It wasn't until both Tiger's parents began to observe his unusual interest in the game that they began to indulge his passion for the sport. In the early years of Tiger's development, Earl served exclusively as his coach. Earl was able to teach him the fundamentals of the game—grip, stance and the basics of the swing—so that Tiger had a solid grounding from the beginning. But the more significant direct contribution to his son's evolution as a champion golfer was in the mental aspects of the game. Earl would play little games with young Tiger to test his ability to eliminate mental and physical distractions. For example, Earl would wait until his son was in the middle of his backswing and drop a golf ball, or rattle some change in his pocket, to try and disrupt his concentration. Sometimes Tiger would get annoyed, but indicative of the unique relationship the two had forged, Earl would leave it up to Tiger to determine when he had gone too far. Tiger has talked about his father's early techniques: "...it was pretty tough but, it was never in a bad-natured way. It was always in a way that he never degraded you as a person, just what you did and your actions. He would never get into your personality."[7]

Games like these were part of a program to prepare Tiger for not only the physical challenges of golf, but also the psychological obstacles to winning. Tiger was constantly and understandably trying to challenge his father to test his skill against his teacher's. They would have driving contests during which Tiger would routinely out drive his father by twenty yards. However Earl would insist that the ball had to stop in the fairway to be counted, sometimes a matter of inches. Both Tiger's parents intentionally contributed to what Earl has referred to a "dark side, a coldness..."[8] in his son. His mother reinforced that idea. While she wouldn't tolerate him losing his temper on the golf course, she made it clear that the objective was to win. "I tell Tiger, 'When you are ahead, don't take it easy, kill them,'" she said, "'After the finish, then be a sportsman.'"[9]

By 1979, stories of Tiger's precociousness began to circulate, and eventually Tiger's mother called Jim Hill, a former football player and local Los Angeles sports television reporter, and asked him to come out to the Navy course to watch Tiger play. Hill brought along a camera crew and produced a news piece featuring the four-year-old Tiger. Subsequently Tiger appeared on *That's Incredible* with Minnesota Vikings quarterback Fran Tarkenton, *The Mike Douglas Show* with comedian Bob Hope and *The Tonight Show with Johnny Carson*. When he was seven he played an exhibition match with Sam Snead. The first notable mention of him in a national magazine was a one paragraph item in the November 1981 issue of *Golf Digest* entitled "5-Year-Old Tiger: He's Incredible."[10] This kind of publicity and adulation for a five year old might have been a problem for many kids. However, the constant nurturing of Tiger's parents apparently kept him immune from developing a large ego. And he did not appear at all intimidated by the pressure of talking in front of large groups of people, let alone the cameras broadcasting to a national audience. When Bob Hope asked the young golfing prodigy if he had any money, jokingly implying that they were going to bet on their competition, two-year-old Tiger cleverly moved his ball closer to the hole and tapped it into the cup.

Earl Woods tells the story of the four-year-old Tiger coming off the golf course with a pocket full of quarters. He had won them by putting for quarters with some older boys. His father reprimanded him and told him that he shouldn't be gambling for quarters anymore. Later his father saw him with a fist full of dollar bills and asked where they came from. Not wanting to disobey his father, the young golfer had been playing a skins game, for folding money—not putting for quarters. His father told him to cease playing for money in the future—unless he was his partner.[11]

While he was an accomplished amateur golfer, at a certain point Earl Woods felt that he was no longer able to provide the advanced training Tiger required. So he tried to find a professional who would work with Tiger, and who would not be too expensive. Kultida Woods, in search of a course where Tiger would be allowed to play without his father, found the Heartwell Golf Course in Long Beach, a par three public course. When she approached Rudy Duran, an assistant professional there, and asked about someone who could teach her son, he asked to see the boy swing. Duran was amazed: "...I felt he was like Mozart. He was a little shrunken touring pro. If I could have taken Jack Nicklaus and shrunk him down to that size, that's what you would have had. It was genius."[12] Duran agreed to work with Tiger and devised a special "par" for the short course that took into account the limited distance the four-year-old Tiger could hit the ball. Since Tiger was able to play below the adjusted par even at this young age, it significantly bolstered his confidence. Ironically, the apparent discrimination at the Navy course, which led Tiger to the par-3 Heartwell course, forced him to concentrate on his short game at a very early age. Eventually Duran used the young Woods to help him when he did teaching clinics. Tiger had an uncanny understanding of the golf swing, and even at his age he was able to point out swing flaws in other golfers.

Subsequently Earl would expose Tiger to a series of professional teach-ers and advisors—later nicknamed "Team Tiger"—each supplying a vital element at the appropriate time to his development. John Anselmo had once been an aspiring tournament golf professional who lost his periph-eral vision after being struck by a golf ball. He turned to teaching golf and was working at the Meadowlark Golf Club in Huntington Beach, California, when Earl Woods sought him out to teach his son in 1986. "I saw so much rhythm and balance, even when he was ten. I was awed by it. I knew even at the time he was special. It's like destiny. I was so excited to have been a part of the Tiger team."[13] Anselmo would be actively involved in Tiger's instruction for about seven years.

Another crucial person who contributed to evolution of Tiger Woods when Tiger was 14 was Jay Brunza. Earl Woods met and played with then Commander Brunza, USN, at the Navy course in Cypress. Brunza, a sports psychologist who had worked with Naval Academy athletes to help them concentrate, and an avid golfer, would play an important role in the developing Tiger's unprecedented power of concentration on the golf course. Through hypnosis and other mind tricks, Brunza was able to sharpen Woods's ability to focus on the task at hand even when faced with the most intense pressure. He also occasionally caddied for Woods through his junior career.[14]

Despite the fact that Tiger was considered special by so many people, his parents tried to instill in him a sense of proportion regarding his talents. On his first day of kindergarten in September of 1981 at a school with relatively few minority students, he experienced his first brush with overt racism. He was confronted by a group of mostly older white boys who tied him to a tree and taunted him with racial slurs. The incident was handled by the school authorities and the guilty parties were identified and punished. Despite this incident, and due in no small part to economics, his parents were committed to sending him to public schools and overall his experience in school was positive. During kindergarten, his teacher recommended that he skip a grade because she thought he was clearly ahead of most of the class. After considering the prospects, his parents decided that they should leave it up to Tiger to decide. Because he was already competing mainly against older kids in golf, Tiger told them he wanted to stay with his own classmates in school.

No one has been able to provide an explanation of why, even before he was born, Tiger Woods exhibited an almost mystical passion for the game of golf. While even he can't explain it, there are numerous examples of Tiger's obsession with the game. His mother tells how, when he was growing up, the ultimate punishment was to take away his golf clubs. If he had homework to do, he couldn't play golf until it was done. It is tempting to assume that his parents were either overtly or subtly exerting pressure on him to practice. But various observers have concluded that they saw no evidence of such pressure. Jay Brunza commented, "Tiger was pursuing something from intrinsic passion for the game, and wasn't forced to live out somebody else's expectations. If he said 'I'm tired of golf, I want to collect stamps,' his parents would say, 'Fine son,' and walk him down to the post office."[15] He participated in a variety of sports and exhibited exceptional skill in many of them, including baseball, basketball, and cross-country running. But inevitably he dropped any other activities because it was taking time away from practicing and playing golf.

By the time he reached 10 years old, at 4'9" and 81 pounds, he had already won two Junior World Championships (under 10 years old). He continued to maintain an unprecedented competitive record as a child golfer. In addition to a host of local tournaments in and around his home, he won the Optimist International Junior Championship six times, from the ages of 8 through 13. At 13 he finished second in the Insurance Youth Golf Classic National Tournament. By the time he was fourteen he had accumulated over 200 trophies.[16] He carefully constructed a chart with a list in the left hand column of all the major championships (U.S. Open, British Open, Masters, & P.G.A. Championship). In the right column he pasted a cutout picture of Jack Nicklaus, and his age when he first won each of these tournaments. It was not only his goal to win all the major championships, but also to do it at an earlier age than his idol.

In interviews, Tiger has repeatedly emphasized his relatively normal teenage years. However, there are countless examples of how his adolescence deviated from the norm. He refused to participate in Little League baseball because it would take too much time away from practicing and playing golf. During the summer between the seventh and eighth grade, one of his female classmates asked him out on a date; he declined for the same reason. The only consistently normal aspect of his teenage behavior was his diet. He exhibited a great interest in McDonald's, Taco Bell, and pizza. He also watched his share of television, favoring *The Simpsons* and professional wrestling.

TIGER IN SCHOOL

Tiger Woods attended Orangeview Junior High School in Cypress, and then Western High School in Anaheim, where Don Crosby was his coach. Crosby recalls the first time he saw Tiger practicing at the Navy course at Los Alimitos, where his high school golf team practiced. He was fascinated by this young, slight junior high school boy hitting golf balls at the practice range by himself for hours. He tried to use the young Woods as an example to his team of the value of practice. Their response was they preferred practicing while they played. He would see Woods on the practice tee when they teed off and he'd still be there when they finished several hours later. He describes his feelings when he learned there might be a chance that Tiger Woods would enroll at Western High:

One day in 1990, my number-one player casually said to me, 'Coach, Tiger Woods lives in my neighborhood.' I stopped cold. 'Same housing tract as you?' I said, afraid to even think what I'm thinking. 'Yeah,' he said, 'he lives right around the corner from me.' 'Same Tiger Woods as we saw at Los Alimitos, not some other kid coincidentally named Tiger Woods?' I asked, just to make sure this wasn't some cruel joke. 'Yeah, coach, the Tiger Woods.' Well, he might as well have told me Johnny Unitas, Mickey Mantle and Michael Jordan were going to play for Western High. This was a coach's dream...[17]

Barring a last-minute redistricting, owing to declining enrollment occurring during the late 80s and early 90s in the district, Crosby allowed himself the luxury of contemplating the impact of Tiger Woods on his golf team's fortunes. The impact was instant and unprecedented.

Tiger played varsity golf all four years at Western High, despite the fact that by his senior year he was being invited to and occasionally playing in PGA tournaments that precluded playing the high school matches. He won the Southern Section California Interscholastic Federation Championship four times, culminating with a 30 on the back nine of the final round in his senior year. High school golf matches are usually nine-hole medal (stroke) play competitions, with points awarded for each of the two-player matches. Over his four-year high school golf career, Tiger Woods managed to score an amazing 36 strokes under par for over 100 nine-hole matches.

During his sophomore year, Western High lost the conference team championship to Valencia High by one stroke, after Tiger, unaware of its importance, nonchalantly missed a two-foot putt. Coach Crosby reminded Woods' teammates that Tiger hadn't lost the title; it was a team loss. However, undoubtedly the experience was an important lesson about maintaining concentration for the young Woods.

The unprecedented attention this young golfer received throughout his life had hardly been missed by college golf coaches throughout the country. *Sports Illustrated* featured Tiger in its "In The Crowd" feature on September 24, 1990, "...Tiger Woods, Cypress, Calif. Tiger, 14, shot a two under 286 for 72 holes to win a national junior golf tournament at Ridgles Country Club in Forth Worth. He has won five Junior World Titles, including the Optimist International in San Diego last July."[18]

Wally Goodwin, the coach of the Stanford University golf team, noticed the article and sent a letter indicating his interest in having Tiger consider attending Stanford. He was considerably impressed when he received a return letter from the 13-year-old seventh grader, thanking him for his interest and telling him that his junior high school GPA was 3.86, and that he was starting an exercise program to help fill out his 5'9", 120-pound physique. Goodwin was somewhat taken aback at the composition of the letter and the quality of the prose that clearly seemed beyond the skills of most thirteen year olds. He told some of his players that this letter from a minority kid in Los Angeles and they could learn something from his example.

Tiger was recruited by dozens of colleges and universities, but most intensely by Stanford, Arizona State, Virginia, Arizona, and Nevada–Las Vegas. Eventually Tiger narrowed his college choices down to University of Nevada-Las Vegas and Stanford. His high school coach, Don Crosby, described the first press conference ever held at Western High School to announce Tiger's collegiate intentions. There were two baseball caps on the table in front of Tiger and finally he placed the UNLV hat under the table. There was a rule that students could only wear Western "Pioneer" hats in school to avoid potential conflict between gang affiliations. The photographers clamored for Tiger to put on the Stanford hat, and finally the principal made an exception to the rule for that one day.[19]

Tiger had the choice of virtually any college he wanted to attend since, in addition to his golfing prowess, he had always been a good student. He owed this academic success mainly to the influence of his parents, particularly his mother. He was regularly on the honor roll and belonged to the National Honor Society. In his senior year he was named the 1993 Dial High School Athlete Scholar of the United States.

The unremarkable backgrounds of Tiger Woods's parents certainly didn't foreshadow the creation of a prodigy. Both had endured considerable hardship in arriving at the point in their lives when their only son was born. And while there is clearly not any single influence that led to the phenomenon that is Tiger Woods, the special bond between Tiger and his parents early in his life cannot be minimized when trying to discover the reasons for his success.

NOTES

1. Earl Woods, *Playing Through* (New York: Harper Collins, 1998), 60.

2. National Golf Foundation, http://www.ngf.org/cgi/whofaqa.asp#5.

3. Ibid., 67.

4. Ibid., 70.

5. Tim Rosaforte, *Tiger Woods: The Making of A Champion* (New York: St. Martin's Press, 1997), 17.

6. John Strege, *A Biography of Tiger Woods* (New York: Broadway Books, 1998), 14.

7. *Golf Talk Live*, The Golf Channel, 18 December 1996.

8. Quoted in Strege, 37.

9. Quoted in Rosaforte, 21.

10. *Golf Digest*, November, 1980: 15.

11. Strege, 15.

12. Quoted in Strege, 16.

13. Quoted in Strege, 34.

14. Rosaforte 25.

15. Quoted in Bill Gutman, *Tiger Woods: A Biography* (New York: Pocket Books, 1997), 28.

16. Nicholas Edwards, *Tiger Woods: An American Master* (New York: Scholastic Inc., 1997), 18.

17. Don Crosby, *"Tiger Woods Made Me Look Like A Genius"* (Kansas City: McMeel Publishing, 2000), 11.

18. *Sports Illustrated*, 24 September 1990: 10.

19. Don Crosby, 132–133.

Chapter 2

PARENTS

Probably the most recognized nickname in the world of sports is Tiger. However, his real name is Eldrick Woods. And it is worth noting that his mother insisted on that name starting with the letter E for Earl, and ending with the letter K, for Kutilda, so that "he would always know that he was surrounded by his parents."[1] In an age when most references to parents' involvement with their talented offspring are negative, Tiger Woods and his parents have certainly managed to convey a very positive example of how to nurture a sports prodigy. There is no evidence that they started out with that objective.

EARL

While both parents were influential and contributed some element to the overall development of Tiger Woods, there's no doubt that Earl Woods provided the most visible presence both with Tiger as well as the public through the media. It was because of Earl's interest in golf that Tiger was introduced to the sport, and he has by far been more accessible than his wife. There seems little doubt that all of Earl's experiences before the birth of Tiger Woods had a significant impact on how he dealt with this potential superstar athlete.

Pinning down exact times and dates concerning the life of Earl Woods is not easy considering this man was born and grew up in the middle of America in the middle of the twentieth century. He has demonstrated a colossal inability to remember specific dates and times of what most people would consider significant events in their lives. However, because

of the overwhelming interest in his son, and the universally acknowl-
edged impact Earl had on his son's development, many reporters have
devoted countless hours tracking down confirmation of some of Earl's
exploits. For example, when asked when he was married to his second
wife, Earl couldn't remember the date. The influence of the army on Earl's
life is undeniable, and especially the two tours of duty that he served.
However, when *Golf Digest* reporter Tom Callahan asked when he served
in Vietnam, Earl couldn't remember the dates. For any veteran, this
seemed implausible, so marine veteran Callahan embarked on a journey
into Earl's military files, compliments of the Freedom of Information Act,
and discovered that he had in fact served in Vietnam at two different
times.[2] Because of this, although this book will contain ample references
to Earl's autobiography, *Playing Through*, the information about Earl's life
has been confirmed or corroborated as much as possible.

Kansas Years

Earl Dennison Woods was born in Manhattan, Kansas on March
5, 1932 into a family of six children. As the youngest child of Maude
and Miles Woods, he grew up in what would today be called modest
circumstances. While Earl doesn't recall being poor, he remembers the
local Rotary Club delivering food baskets to his family on Thanksgiving
days. He describes his childhood as being happy, despite being aware that
they did not have plenty. One enduring memory he has is of the best
Christmas present he received, a twenty-five cent kite. Earl Woods grew
up in Kansas at a time when blacks had not yet gained, even de jure, the
full rights of citizenship in America.

His father was a brick mason who once had aspirations to play professional baseball, and taught Earl the value of hard manual labor. In
addition to his principal job, he worked part time as a gardener and ran
the scoreboard at a local baseball field on weekends. Earl occasionally
accompanied his father to help him work the scoreboard. Not inciden-
tally, the field was reserved for white teams only, namely teams from the
Ban Johnson League which tried for a time to challenge the American
and National Leagues. From all descriptions of Earl's father, their relationship was more dependent on their love of baseball than conversation
and intellectualizing.

Maude Woods was a college graduate who spent her entire life doing
domestic work because there were few opportunities for educated black
women in Depression-era Kansas, or anyplace else in America, for
that matter. According to Earl's recollection it was his mother who

instilled most of the values that today are ascribed to his youngest son. Apparently his mother was a soft-spoken woman who nevertheless had strong opinions and stated them. There seems to be no question that her own education had a great effect on her children in their early life. She valued education and demanded that her children study and attain good grades. Earl talks about how he once had several bad conduct reports from school, and how his mother went in to see the teacher and rather than challenge the teacher, she implored him to give Earl more work. Earl distinguishes between the phrases his mother used such as "pride" and "being responsible for your own actions" and our contemporary emphasis on "positive self image" and concern about children's "damaged egos." Undoubtedly her training in education provided both the will and ability to teach her children to speak and write properly, and she would not tolerate sloppy grammar. Earl tells a story of how, when he was a child, he and the black community looked up to heavy-weight boxing champion Joe Louis. Coincidentally, Joe Louis was a close friend of one of the Woods's neighbors, Mr. Fred Harrison. Louis was stationed at Fort Riley and would occasionally visit the neighborhood, and Earl got to meet him personally. He recalls his mother's comments after that meeting, "Don't you dare talk the way Joe Louis talks when you grow up! I want you to get an education, and I want you to speak properly."[3]

Interestingly, Earl's father was a Baptist and his mother was a Methodist, and while he participated actively in religious events throughout his early childhood, there was apparently never any pressure to commit to one or the other sect. So while there is no question that religion played a role in his upbringing, there was not any hard emphasis on which religion was "right."

The considerable influence exerted on Earl by his parents is very apparent in light of the fact that they died when he was relatively young and he was, for the most part, raised by his oldest sister, Hattie. When Earl was 11, his father died of a stroke. At around the same time, Earl's older brother Miles enlisted in the air force, leaving Earl as the oldest male in the house. Earl refers to this moment as a significant turning point in his life, from childhood to manhood. He was forced to watch his mother grieve over the loss of his father, and die herself of a stroke two years later. He describes his mother's funeral when distant relatives gathered and spoke in hushed tones in corners at the funeral home trying to determine what would become of Earl and his sisters and brothers. He notes with obvious pride, when his 29-year-old sister Hattie stated to the relatives, "We are not going to be separated. We will stay in this house. I will raise everybody."[4]

Despite the nontraditional arrangement in Earl's family, he had a fairly normal upbringing through high school. He notes in his book that the responsibilities in the house were delegated pretty much along gender lines which led to his lifelong ideas about male/female roles, asserting that "...today I could have 10 vacuum cleaners and I still wouldn't touch them."[5] As a teenager he played American Legion baseball on a white team, and his family traveled all over the state to watch him play. Earl was a catcher and was close to the stands where bigots would shout insults, frequently shouting racial epithets. His family had to endure these indignities and remain composed.

One incident in high school exemplifies the general racist environment of postwar Kansas. Earl was a finalist for the prom king contest, and school administrators were anticipating in advance the prospects of a black king having to kiss a white queen. According to Earl the results were rigged and the so-called problem averted.

Graduating high school presented the young Earl Woods with a dilemma about what direction he would go in his life. Earl was offered a scholarship to play baseball at nearby Kansas State University. His mother had always hoped throughout her brief life that he would graduate from college. So Earl enrolled and rode his bicycle the four miles to the university every day. He diligently tried to maintain his studies while he devoted most of his time to his real love—playing baseball. Miles Woods had aspirations of Earl playing baseball in the Negro Leagues, specifically for the local Kansas City Monarchs. During his first year in college, despite the fact that the Negro Leagues would soon be on the wane (Jackie Robinson broke the color line in major-league baseball in 1947), Earl was offered a contract with the team, which would have been the fulfillment of his father's dream. It was becoming increasingly more difficult for Earl to study and play baseball, and accepting the contract with the Monarchs would have eliminated any possibility of his finishing college. A decision had to be made. Apparently Maude's voice from the grave was the strongest, as Earl decided to bypass the baseball contract and dedicate himself to finishing college.

While continuing to play baseball for Kansas State, he majored in psychology. Earl was a better-than-average baseball player and while at Kansas State he established some racial firsts of his own. He was not only the first African American baseball player at Kansas State, but also in what was then the Big 7 Conference.[6] Playing baseball and going to college was an important choice, however it was another decision he made that would eventually have an even greater impact on the rest of his life.

Earl's sister Hattie married a World War II veteran, Jesse Spearman, who was a premed student at Kansas State. As an officer, he sent all his pay home to be put away to help finance his medical education. When he returned from the war he found out that his brother had spent all the money. In what must have been an extraordinary demonstration of discipline and dedication, considering the prevalent racial discrimination of the times, Jesse somehow managed to work his way through college and medical school, eventually becoming a gynecologist. Jesse served as the major male figure in Earl's life when he was in college. It was Jesse who convinced Earl to consider signing up for advanced ROTC at Kansas State, and even though he had missed the deadline, the officer in charge, recognizing Earl as the only black player on the baseball team, made an exception and accepted him.

Army Years

After graduating from Kansas State and accepting a commission in the United States Army, Earl played semiprofessional baseball while waiting to be called to active duty. His first assignment took him to Germany, where he encountered his first personality conflict with a superior officer that had clear racial overtones. After answering a question in what the officer obviously considered a flippant manner, Earl was confronted by the following outburst: "You're one of those smart niggers. We don't have any place for people like you in the army. I'm going to make damn sure that you don't stay."[7]

In the military there is a distinct delineation between Regular Army Military Academy graduate officers and reserve officers commissioned by other means (ROTC, Officer Candidate School, direct commissions). Non-academy officers tend to be looked down upon by the West Pointers, and even though President Harry Truman had officially outlawed discrimination in the military in 1948, the reality of the newly-integrated units was not fully accepted by every officer. Early in his career, Earl mainly served in administrative positions, and at least partially because of the racial situation he was not put in positions that would enhance his opportunities for promotion. In order to facilitate promotions, particularly in the infantry branch, an officer must serve time as a unit commander. A lieutenant is usually designated a platoon leader, a captain serves as company commander, and so on up the line.

The Vietnam War represents a significant event in the life of Earl Woods. It was this war that precipitated his meeting two people who would exert a considerable amount of influence on him, and contribute immeasurably to the evolution of Tiger Woods. While Earl couldn't exactly pinpoint when he served in Vietnam, the record indicates he served two tours of duty there, from February 12, 1962 to February 24, 1963, and then again from August 15, 1970 to August 13, 1971. His first duty in Vietnam was as a regular infantry officer and from what information is available, he served in administrative positions. He subsequently returned to the United States, and after an assignment to Thailand he made the unorthodox decision, at the age of 35 to volunteer for Special Forces training.

Beginning in 1961, when President John Kennedy authorized the adoption of the Green Beret as the official headgear of all Special Forces, this elite unit of the army became associated with the highest levels of courage and achievement in the United States military.[8] The qualifications for Special Forces training were very strict, and the prospects of a 35-year-old officer meeting those standards were slim. However, Earl Woods had determined that Special Forces units were the one place in the army he felt he would be judged completely on his ability to complete his mission. As a former athlete, Earl had little trouble with the physical aspects of training. He first completed airborne jump training at Fort Benning, Georgia. As the ranking officer in the jump school class, he was called upon to serve as an example to the other soldiers. Earl tells of an incident when he led his class in a pull up exercise in subfreezing cold, being the first to jump up and take the cold metal bar, covered in ice.[9] After jump school Earl was briefly assigned as the briefing officer at the Vietnam Village at Fort Bragg, while the John Wayne movie *Green Berets* was being filmed. Indicative of the intensity of training, Earl recounts an exercise at survival school in Alaska when the candidates were required to make a forced march across 20 miles of frozen tundra. One of the soldiers couldn't make it and told Captain Woods that he needed help. Earl told the soldier that he had two choices: to keep up with the rest of the party, or be found frozen in a snow because there was no way that a truck was going to come out to get him. The soldier caught up.[10]

Tiger "One"

After completing Special Forces training, Earl served a second tour in Vietnam. This time he would not be behind a desk in Saigon. As a Special Forces commander, he would be in charge of a Special Forces team made up of 12 soldiers. Earl had a number of brushes with death, and was awarded the Vietnamese Silver Star for unspecified acts of bravery.[11]

More importantly, Earl met and befriended Lieutenant Colonel Vuong Dang Phong, Deputy Chief of Binh Thuan Province, to whom Earl was assigned as advisor. Their assignment was to visit relocation villages in which the U.S. was intent upon convincing the "hearts and minds" of the Vietnamese people to reject the communist ideology in favor of democracy. Earl experienced the same fears as the rest of the American soldiers assigned to Vietnam: it was impossible to determine who the enemy was. In these villages it was impossible to know who had malicious intent toward the Americans and the Vietnamese who collaborated with the Americans. Children as young as eight or nine years old were trained to plant munitions to harm their enemies. It was not uncommon to find young boys selling powerful, pure heroin for fifty cents to GIs with the hope of getting them hooked on the drug.[12] It was a new kind of war and the North Vietnamese army and the insurgent Vietcong represented an entirely new kind of warfare.

Under the extreme pressure of the situation Earl Woods developed a strong bond with this slight (5'5" tall) South Vietnamese officer. Beyond his deep respect for Col. Phong's innate intelligence and thoroughly professional competence as a military officer, Earl credits Phong with several instances where he literally saved his life. While Earl has occasionally justified these brushes with death as some kind of cosmic plan preparing him for his eventual role as the father of Tiger Woods, there seems to be no question that these incidents helped strengthen the relationship between these two men and, for the purposes of tracing the impact they would have on his son, are worth recounting.

Earl recounts an incident on a mission when he asked Col. Phong to call in helicopter fire support for his South Vietnamese troops. The mission was beyond the capabilities of the South Vietnamese units, so only Earl could request the support. The ground was dusty, and while completely engaged in the coordinating the gunfire from the helicopters, he noticed Col. Phong hollering at him from a ditch beside the dike of a rice paddy. Oblivious to anything but his mission he noticed a pile of dirt to his right and suddenly it was gone. There was also a pile of dirt to his left and suddenly it was gone, too. Phong continued to holler, but Earl, unable to understand what Phong wanted, continued to direct the gun ships. The helicopters finished their mission, and Earl finally joined Phong in the ditch, and asked what he wanted. Phong replied: "You are the coolest adviser I have ever had in my life. A sniper bracketed you. The first shot went to your right. The second shot went to your left. And I expected the third shot to go right through your chest. That's what I was trying to tell you."[13]

A little while later Earl found a quiet bamboo thicket to get some much needed rest. He was awakened by Phong, who told him to stay perfectly still. The bamboo viper is apparently one of the most poisonous snakes in the world, and one had made his way down the bamboo to hang inches from Earl's face. In what Earl later described as another unexplained reason for his life being spared, the viper retreated back into the bamboo thicket.

Because of his tenacious reputation on the battlefield and his unrestrained commitment to the mission and his troops, Earl nicknamed Col. Phong "Tiger," the most feared and courageous animal in the jungles of Vietnam. These two men from widely different cultures were able to forge a relationship that went beyond professional respect. In their off hours, Earl introduced Phong to the world of jazz music, chili, and tennis, and Phong taught Earl the rudiments of Eastern philosophy and religion. The two men spent many hours drinking in Earl's quarters, nicknamed the "Blue Room," painted infantry blue, the color of Earl's service branch. When Saigon fell in 1975, Earl vowed that if he ever had another son (by this time he was remarried) he would name him Tiger in honor of his comrade in arms.

Except for the fact that Earl would father the most heralded professional golfer in the world, the relationship between these two men would probably have been forgotten as one of the many cross-cultural friendships precipitated by war. Earl lost all contact with Phong when he left Vietnam in 1971. In subsequent years he made attempts through missing-person services in New York City to find out what happened to his friend after the fall of Saigon in 1975. But it wasn't until Tiger became an international celebrity that he was able to make any serious progress toward determining Phong's fate. Earl enlisted the services of several detective agencies to try and find out what happened to Phong after they lost touch. Ironically, it wasn't until Tom Callahan, a reporter for *Golf Digest* magazine, went on a journalistic adventure to find out what happened to Tiger One, that the true story emerged.

Callahan, initially skeptical about Earl's fuzzy memory with regard to his military career, in particular his service in Vietnam, began research on an article for his magazine in 1996. Under the guise of doing an article on a new golf course in Vietnam, designed by prominent international golfer Nick Faldo, Callahan managed to acquire a visa to visit Ho Chi Minh City, formerly Saigon. He had been warned to bypass the Ministry of Foreign Affairs if he didn't want to be "handled" by the local bureaucrats, so he hired a driver, Thanh, and his sister Thuy, who suggested that they start the search at the Pagoda of Vinh-Nghiem. Callahan was unable to acquire any concrete evidence about the fate of Phong, but he did gather information that eventually led to the answer. It turned out that the ostensible reason for the trip, an article about the new golf course, turned out to reap the most fruitful benefit of the trip to Vietnam. When playing the course, one of his playing companions was Flower, a North Vietnamese businesswoman who suggested that Callahan place an ad in a Vietnamese-American newspaper asking for information about Earl's friend. It was apparent that the government wasn't going to help him since he was reprimanded during a call from the ministry in Hanoi for not reporting to the ministry in Ho Chi Minh City.

After returning to America and placing some ads in local Vietnamese-American press, Callahan received a phone call from a man who connected Col. Phong's name with that of Earl Woods and the blue room. Despite the language barriers, through several calls to Vietnam, and the realization that Earl had been mistaken about Phong's first name—it was Vuong, not Nguyen. This was understandable since Nguyen is comparable to the name Bob in America. Through Callahan's golf mate, Flower, contact was made with the family of Vuong Dang Phong, also known as Tiger One.

The story that emerged confirmed the legacy of Tiger One. He surrendered to the Communists on June 15, 1975, and was sent to a reeducation camp in Vinh Phu. The first year he managed to send a letter to his family of nine children. His family heard nothing for 10 years until the government informed then that he died in the camp on September 9, 1976.[14]

Ironically, Earl was subsequently to learn that Phong's widow, Lythi Bich Van, had been living in the United States in Tacoma, Washington since 1994, and had no idea who Tiger Woods was. Tom Callahan, through the courtesy of *Golf Digest* magazine, arranged for the two families to meet at Earl's home in Cypress, California. It was an emotional occasion with many tears, recalling the life of Col. Phong. Phong's wife and two of her children met Earl, his wife Kultida, and Tiger, who flew in from Florida to join them. Undoubtedly the friendship between these two military officers had had an indelible impact on both of them, however, given the influence this man had on Earl Woods, his life had spawned probably one of the greatest nicknames in all of sports, and brought some much needed attention to the fate of thousands of other South Vietnamese citizens who had vanished when America withdrew from Vietnam.

Earl's First Family

Divorce in twentieth-century America is not an unusual phenomenon. So it is not especially significant that Earl Woods was married twice.

However, in order to thoroughly examine the forces that shaped Tiger Woods, it is important to explore the factors that led Earl to marry right out of college and father three children, divorce and remarry a woman of a completely different cultural background, and most important, father a son at the age of 43.

As with other aspects of Earl's life, it has been difficult to pin down exact dates and sequences for various events. This was also the case regarding his marital history. Earl admits in his autobiography that he made a number of mistakes regarding the choice of his first wife, Barbara Hart, whom he married in 1954.[15] Eventually they had three children, two boys (Earl and Kevin) and a girl (Royce). Several different sources give evidence of different dates for their divorce, but it appears that the date was in 1966. Earl openly admits that many of the factors that led to his divorce were his fault. He notes that the pressures of being a new officer at a new post in Germany were only exacerbated when he decided to bring his new wife along. The army made no accommodations for housing junior officer's families, and consequently they had to pay rent from his modest lieutenant's salary. Adding to the stress undoubtedly was the racial situation in Germany at the time. The Germans were not used to seeing black men, and certainly not black women, and some white GIs had told outrageous stories about black people thereby causing the locals to look with curiosity at this young black couple.

When they returned to the United States, it apparently didn't get any better. Earl was constantly away from his family, and he admits that he didn't pay enough attention to the children from his first marriage, and that he considered it a second chance to be able to make up for the mistakes he made with his new son. Through the years, Earl has managed to maintain contact with his first family, and from time to time the children have all lived with him. He notes an incident involving his son Kevin, a natural left-handed batter. Earl returned from an assignment overseas to find Kevin batting right-handed. He told his father that since everybody else seemed to be batting right-handed, he decided to switch.[16] Earl felt that it would not have happened if he had been around to play a more significant role in the children's upbringing.

He refers to the final chapter of his first marriage when he was served with papers filed by his wife in 1996 suing for half of his military retirement pay, retroactively and in the future. In light of the fact that she had remarried, the case was thrown out of court.[17]

KULTIDA

Equally as difficult to pin down as the date of Earl's divorce is the date that he met Tiger's mother Kultida. At some point between his first and second tours in Vietnam—between 1963 and 1970—he was assigned to Bangkok, Thailand. It was there, as a special services officer, he was working as a civilian personnel office attempting to hire 4,000 civilian workers. Earl was accompanied by a white junior officer who answered, "Colonel Woods" when the attractive, petite Thai receptionist asked, "Can I help you?" When Earl returned to talk to the young woman, Kultida Punswad, she was immediately embarrassed to have wrongly assumed that the white officer was Colonel Woods.[18] So their first encounter foreshadowed some of the racial assumptions that would someday mark their son. They made arrangements for a date at nine o'clock. Earl waited at the agreed-upon location, since it would have been impolite for him to go to her house. Kultida never showed up. The next morning Earl was roused out of bed at nine o'clock by Kultida and her chaperone. She had assumed he was talking about morning since she it would not have been appropriate for her to go out that late at night. They eventually did go out to visit a Thai church.

Kultida Punsawad came from a family with considerable commercial standing. Her father owned a tin mine and the family owned a fleet of buses in Bangkok. Tida (as she is known) was brought up in a boarding school as her parents separated when she was five[19] and, like her husband-to-be, she was the product of a several races. She is a mixture of Thai, Chinese, and Caucasian, and practices Buddhism.[20] Young women of her social class were not encouraged by their families to fraternize with American soldiers, and certainly not black soldiers, so the relationship between Earl and Kultida faced obstacles in her native country, let alone the United States. There is no question that this was an unusually self-directed young woman who had her own modern ideas about relationships, despite the fact that many in her family ostracized her. Some of these same qualities become apparent in her role as Tiger's mother, and she must have experienced some form of revenge when she returned to Thailand in 1997 to watch Tiger win the Asian Honda Classic Tournament at the Thai Country Club by 10 strokes. Kultida and her son were hailed as royalty.

Kultida Woods is certainly the least publicized member of what has become known as Team Tiger, the people who now cater to the golfer's needs in all aspects of his life. This quiet woman combines a stern single-mindedness with a spiritual calm that has undoubtedly been a significant influence on her son. Buddhism is the state religion in Thailand, even though there is religious freedom in the country. The philosophy of Buddhism stresses three principal aspects of existence—suffering, impermanence and nonsubstantiality, and without reading too much into the impact of Buddhist philosophy on the eventual ability of Tiger Woods to hit a golf ball, his mother's religious history has certainly had an effect on his personality. So it is probably not too much to assume that since the objective of Buddhist philosophy is to overcome all desire and thereby reach a state of inaction that assures the end of a cycle of rebirth or reincarnation,[21] this emphasis on self-discipline, unfettered determination, and calm has seeped into the psyche of Tiger Woods. When he was nine Kultida took him to Thailand to introduce him to her native country, and a part of his culture. She brought him to a Buddhist monk to analyze a chart she had kept on Tiger's life. Unaware as the monk was of the game of golf, or the accomplishments of Tiger, he told Kultida that Tiger was special child who was destined for leadership. If he went into the military, she was told, he would become a four-star general.[22]

According to the most reliable sources, Earl and Kultida married sometime in 1969. There is some question as to that exact date but whatever the date of the marriage, by 1973 they were living in New York City, where Earl was assigned to Fort Hamilton as a public relations officer. It was around this time that he seriously took up the game of golf.

Earl had been challenged by a fellow officer, and considering himself a pretty decent athlete, he took up the challenge to a golf match. He was soundly defeated, but rather than shun the game, he embraced it. He dedicated himself to perfecting his golf swing and devoted most of his leisure time to practicing golf. He made a commitment to a rematch with this officer before he left the service in less than a year. Earl requested a rematch and shot a career best round of 84 and won the match.[23] Less than any natural physical ability, it was this indomitable will to win that was the most lasting legacy Earl Woods imparted to his son Tiger.

Following his retirement from the Army in 1974, Earl and Kultida moved to California, ostensibly to be closer to his three children. With the birth of Tiger, both parents devoted all their energies to their new son, and Earl admits that this unbridled dedication to the well-being of Tiger had its effects on the marriage. While they remain married, they live in separate residences, and live separate lives, except for Tiger. While Kultida has not spoken publicly about the relationship, Earl summarized the state of their marriage in his autobiography: "Today, we are the best of friends, have a beautiful amicable relationship and ardently follow Tiger's development and progress every step of the way, still fully supportive. She has her home, I have mine."[24]

Each parent played different roles in the raising of Tiger Woods. While it was Earl who provided the early introduction to both the physical and psychological rudiments of the game of golf, it was Kultida who provided the environment of discipline and strong work ethic, and made significant sacrifices to make sure Tiger was able to display his prodigal gifts on the golf course.

NOTES

1. Quoted in Earl Woods, *Playing Through* (New York: HarperCollins, 1998), xi.

2. David Owen, *The Chosen One* (New York: Simon & Schuster, 2001), 57.

3. Quoted in Woods, 4.

4. Quoted in Ibid., 13.

5. Quoted in Ibid., 14.

6. This conference became the Big 8 in 1959 and the Big 12 in 1996.

7. Quoted in Ibid., 26.

8. "History of Special Forces, 1961–1971," Department of Army Publication, 1989, http://www.specialoperations.com/Army/Special_Forces/default.html.

9. Woods, 30.

10. Ibid., 31.

11. Tom Callahan, *In Search of Tiger* (New York: Crown Publisher, 2003), 2.

12. Woods, 33.

13. Quoted in Ibid., 36.

14. Callahan, 2.

15. Woods, 44.

16. Ibid., 47.

17. Ibid., 50.

18. Ibid., 54.

19. Gary Smith, "The Chosen One," *Chasing Tiger*, ed. Glenn Stout (Cambridge: Da Capo, 2002), 59.

20. Curt Sampson, *Chasing Tiger* (New York: Atria, 2002), 6.

21. Thanapol Chadchaidee, *Buddhism in Thailand*, 28 December 2004, http://sunsite.au.ac.th/thailand/buddism/.

22. John Strege, *A Biography of Tiger Woods* (New York: Broadway Books, 1998), 25–26.

23. Strege, 11.

24. Woods, 63.

Chapter 3

EARLY COMPETITION

JUNIOR CAREER

Tiger Woods was not the first sports child prodigy to capture the imagination of the American public. What made him unique was the fact that he was a child of color, and that he was competing in a sport that was generally reserved for white children who had the advantage of early access to facilities and coaching, usually in connection with a private club or public courses in exclusive neighborhoods. Golf is the last American sport to actively seek and embrace minority players. Tennis, another sport born of privilege, had already had several black stars by the 1960s, due mostly to the relative accessibility of public courts, the international appeal, and the somewhat blurred line between the amateur and professional versions of the sport until 1968. As will be examined in detail in Chapter 4, it wasn't until 1961 that black golfers were allowed to play regularly on the PGA Tour. Consequently the motivation to pursue a professional career in golf for minorities was limited.

Baseball, basketball and football had a head start in organizing youth sports because of the great number of kids playing those sports. What amounted to a minor league system developed, which would start kids as young as seven not only learning the rudimentary skills of these sports, but also giving them the opportunity to compete locally, regionally, and eventually on a national scale. The high visibility of professional leagues in these sports, showcasing an increasing number of minorities, motivated young minority athletes and their parents to gravitate toward these sports.

When Tiger Woods began at age seven to participate in the junior golf program in Southern California, there were already enough highly organized tournaments to constitute what could only be called a "tour." This tour consisted of 30 tournaments, with upwards of 100 kids playing in each.[1] By the mid 1980s junior golf had expanded to provide a circuit of highly organized tournaments that attracted talented young golfers from all over the world. The American Junior Golf Association (AJGA) is the organization that controls most of those tournaments.

While there were many national junior tournaments of varying degrees of importance, each summer Tiger geared up for the United States Junior Championship, staged by the United States Golf Association. The USGA is the preeminent golf organization in America. In addition to writing the Rules of Golf in collaboration with the British Royal and Ancient Golf Club, the USGA conducts national championships at all levels. Because of the long history and tradition of the organization—it was formed in 1894—and the normally high quality field of players their tournaments attract, the USGA events are considered to be the most prestigious in golf. The U.S. Amateur Championship and the U.S. Open were first conducted in 1895, and players from all over the world attempt to qualify for this tournament. Before he graduated from junior golf, Tiger would become the only male ever to win three U.S. Junior Championships, and each time in dramatic fashion on the 18th or 19th holes.[2] However, being a major success on the junior golf circuit is not an automatic indicator of future success in professional golf. For example, of the six players who won the U.S. Junior Championship before Tiger only three—Gary Koch, Jack Renner and Willie Wood—ever went on to win a PGA tournament.[3]

The evolution of what could now be called a youth sports culture paralleled a significant change in parenting. Where once kids were left to their own devices to entertain themselves, parents now feel it is necessary to provide a never-ending series of options to occupy their children. Whereas kids used to climb trees, run, and make up their own games, they are more and more homebound, watching television and playing video games. When they do participate in physical activities, they are tending to become more and more specialized. So rather than seeing good athletes, we're producing good baseball players.[4] But beyond the physical consequences of this new trend, it is still to be determined what havoc we will have wreaked with the emotional development of this generation of athletes.

It is interesting that one of the most significant and arguably most insidious examples of this new emphasis on early development of athletic talent was prompted by a company that would play a significant role in Tiger Woods's adult career. International Management Group (IMG) was the brainchild of the late Mark McCormick. In the early 1960s McCormick, an attorney, was doing some legal work for Arnold Palmer. Up to this time, athletes had business managers, not agents. McCormick, convinced of Palmer's earning potential, became his agent and made him a multimillionaire, above and beyond whatever he earned playing golf. McCormick is generally considered to be the first true sports agent. In short order he enlisted Jack Nicklaus and Gary Player as clients and eventually developed IMG into an international business that not only represented athletes but also created and ran major sports events. Beyond that, IMG formed IMG Academies in Bradenton, Florida. Originally dedicated exclusively to tennis, under the watchful eye of Nick Bollettieri, who coached Andre Aggasi and Maria Sharapova, among others, the Academy now provides training for young athletes in other sports such as golf, baseball, basketball and soccer. Generally one or the other, or both parents move to the Bradenton area. The Academy makes available condominiums for sale on the grounds for families for $310,000 and combines athletic training with an academic program for middle and high school students. The cost is $30,000 for students who board on campus.[5]

These parents are attracted by the possibility of college scholarships, and the lure of a professional career. Today there is considerable money to be made in all sports beyond the multimillion-dollar salaries because of product endorsement. But it was golf that paved the way for the other sports because of IMG. The reason is that while the audience for golf is relatively small in comparison to the other major sports, the audience is relatively educated and wealthy, and has corporate connections. Also, except for tennis, there's less opportunity to sell equipment for the sport to the football or baseball fan, while golf has a gigantic market.

The question always facing parents who have children with the desire and physical abilities to compete in sports, is whether the parents are encouraging participation for the kids or for themselves? In the case of Tiger Woods there seems little doubt that he wanted to play golf.

Much has been written and speculated about the extent to which Tiger Woods's parents imposed their will on his to produce such a prodigy. The situation has been somewhat clouded by the fact that most of the journalists and writers who have stated opinions on the subject are only witness to the creation of the Tiger Woods phenomenon. Those people who actually participated in his development, it can be argued, now have a vested interest in presenting and perpetuating a positive image of that history. In reviewing the material that has been written about the upbringing of Tiger Woods, there is a general consensus that he was a model junior athlete. Trying to ascertain what made him that way is another question. From his earliest years he not only demonstrated unusual skill at playing golf, but he developed a competitive desire to win that cannot be ascribed to any one source.

EARLY TRAINING

From the start, it must be stated that this was not an ordinary child when it came to golf. As was noted in Chapter 1, even the baby Tiger had an unprecedented attraction to the sport and, unlike most kids, eschewed what would be considered normal diversions. Comparisons have been made to other child prodigies such as Wolfgang Amadeus Mozart, and it's hard to resist the temptation to ascribe supernatural characteristics to this young child. Both had strong father figures, who had to strain to support the creative activities of their sons.[6] Admittedly we're talking about golf, not symphonic music that has remained in the public consciousness for over two hundred years, but the characteristics are similar, and given the amazing accomplishments of the young Tiger Woods, there is no question that he possessed motivation that was well beyond the capabilities of his, or any parents to create. His precociousness on the golf course was surpassed only by the maturity he demonstrated even as a junior golfer.

From all information that the author has been able to review concerning the junior golf career of Tiger Woods, there seems to be no indication that his parents put any extra pressure on him to excel in golf. While at times it is difficult to separate what are the wishes of the son and the wishes of the father, it seems impossible that anyone, even Earl Woods, could have been persuasive enough to make this young child want to play golf at such a competitive level. But there is no question that Earl and Kultida made great sacrifices to nurture the career of Tiger Woods.

Early on when it became apparent that the young Tiger had unusual talent and desire to play competitive golf, his parents realized that it would involve a considerable time commitment as well as substantial financial resources to allow him to compete. Earl talks about how he and Kultida decided that whatever it would cost they would make sacrifices to allow him to develop his God-given talents in golf.[7] Earl describes his method of financing Tiger's junior career by a series of equity loans on his house every summer, which he would pay back during the winter. He estimates it cost about $25,000 to $30,000 a year to pay for expenses related to junior golf tournaments.[8]

While Earl was still working, it was Kultida's responsibility to get Tiger from tournament to tournament, and she quickly became a fixture on the Southern California junior golf circuit. She tried to stay as far in the background as possible, often following Tiger's matches from a distance. Despite her unquestioned loyalty to her son, she always recorded the scores of all the boys in the group and cheered for all the golfers if they made a good shot. There was an incident in one tournament when Tiger missed a short putt and lightly tossed his putter in the air in disgust. This was against AJGA rules. This rule, which was instituted mainly to eliminate swearing and overt demonstrations of temper, was generally not enforced for minor infractions. However, two of the boys in Tiger's group reported him at the end of the round and he was penalized with disqualification. Even though Kultida was convinced that there was some racial motivation on the part of the parents of the boys who reported Tiger's actions, she refused to let Tiger protest the disqualification. Her message to him was clear: Let your clubs speak for you.[9]

It wasn't until Earl retired from his job as a buyer for defense contractor McDonnell Douglas in 1988 that he devoted himself full-time to Tiger's junior golfing career. Because of limited funds, Earl and Tiger usually arrived the night before a tournament and stayed in a motel. Once, Tiger asked his father if there was any way that they could get there earlier so that he might be able to play a practice round before the tournament, like most of the other kids did. That was when Earl and Kultida decided to borrow money to give Tiger the optimum opportunity to compete. Earl decided that he would "go broke if he had to."[10]

The Woods were not like other families who would go on family vacations during holidays and the summer. They would always be traveling to the various junior tournaments. At Christmas, Earl would travel with Tiger to the Junior Invitational Tournament in Miami. At Thanksgiving it was a junior tournament in Tucson, Arizona. Easter was the Woodlands Tournament in Texas. Their lives revolved around Tiger's golf schedule.

Fairly early on Kultida apparently recognized the celebrity potential of her young son, and convinced him to have his eyes examined for contact lenses. The young Tiger was vehemently opposed to the idea and vowed not to put anything into his eyes. She was finally able to convince him that they would be less trouble than glasses, especially on the golf course, and he relented. The future celebrity was also fitted with braces that at least helped perfect the now famous Tiger smile. Earl was quoted as saying, "A million-dollar smile that cost me four thousand dollars."[11]

There were a number of instances when Tiger and his parents confronted one another in the course of his junior playing career. Tiger was leading the Orange Bowl Junior Classic in Miami, missed a short putt and exploded. He then proceeded to give up for the rest of the match, playing in a disinterested fashion—he quit. Following the match, his father, the former military officer and no stranger to dressing down a subordinate in colorful fashion, could be heard over most of the golf course reprimanding his young son. The object of his ire was not the fact that Tiger missed the putt, but that he had given up. Earl reminded Tiger that the game didn't owe him anything, and that he owed it to the game to keep trying, however hopeless the circumstances. Earl Woods referred to Jack Nicklaus, the gauge by which Tiger measured his own accomplishments, and how many times the great golfer continued to grind even when he was not in contention.[12] There is ample evidence that this advice took hold of the young golfer and carried through to his subsequent amateur and professional career. Even the harshest critics of Tiger Woods admit that he continues to try to play his best even when not in contention. In fact, throughout his career, some of his best rounds have come after some of his worst. During the British Open in 2002 at Muirfield he shot an 81 during the rainy, windswept Saturday round—his worst professional tournament round at that point—only to come back the next day and shoot 65,[13] and finish the tournament at even par.

There has been much written about how Tiger dazzled the adults as a young child with his virtually perfect golf swing, and the images persist of this little American child smiling and swinging a golf club like a professional. However, when Tiger began competing in junior tournaments, both he and his father agreed that he would not compete on a level that was beyond his capabilities. When he was 12 and competing in the Yorba Linda (CA) Junior Invitational, he was the overall leader going into the final round, which for 14, 15 and 16 year olds would be played from the blue tees (the longest distances). Tom Sargent, the tournament director, asked Tiger if he wanted to play from the blue tees and thus be eligible for the overall championship. Tiger declined, saying "there'll be plenty of time for that later."[14] So he played from the white tees (shorter distance) and only competed for his age bracket. He did the same thing the next year. Sargent was so impressed with Tiger's maturity that he contacted his friend Wally Goodwin, the golf coach at Stanford, and told him he should start recruiting this young golfer.

There are numerous examples of parents of accomplished developing athletes encouraging them to seek the highest possible levels of competition, despite the possible negative effects. In the National Basketball

Association, high school graduates are occasionally given a special exemption to be drafted by NBA teams. While there have been cases where an athlete has been able to make the physical transition from high school to the NBA, it's not possible to know what the emotional and psychological effects are. So while Lebron James seems to be prospering in professional basketball, it's difficult to gauge the long-range effects. The situation in tennis became so bad that the World Tennis Association imposed minimum age limits, and restricted the number of tournaments in which young players can compete.

A good comparison in golf is the emerging career of with Michele Wei, the teenage prodigy from Hawaii, who has generally avoided playing the junior golf circuit in order to compete in as many LPGA tournaments as sponsor's exemptions would allow. Both Michele and her father have stated that she will learn more competing against professionals than playing in the more traditional junior girls tournaments. One of the many criticisms of Wei in the press, and from other LPGA touring professionals, has been that a young player has to learn to win, and the experience of winning in the junior events would be better preparation for Michele.

Earl developed the idea of enlisting a carefully selected group of people to work with his son to help him perfect all aspects of his golf game, both physical and psychological. When Tiger turned professional, the media quickly picked up on the idea and began referring to this growing group, not always flatteringly, as "Team Tiger." One of those early members of the group was Dr. Jay Brunza, a clinical psychologist for the navy and occasional caddie for Tiger during his junior and amateur career. In addition to carrying his clubs, Jay also worked with Tiger to help him control his mind. He hypnotized Tiger once and told him to hold out his arm straight. Earl, unaware of the hypnosis, tried in vain to move his young son's arm. On another occasion Brunza presented Tiger with a series of focusing techniques, and then arranged a 12-player match, including Tiger. Tiger was five strokes under par, and one of his frustrated opponents drove back to the seventh hole to confront Brunza, claiming he had created a golfing monster.[15] There has been speculation about whether or not Brunza ever hypnotized Tiger before a match. While not indicating that Tiger was ever playing golf in a hypnotic state, he did say that as a professional, "He's now mature enough, too, to put himself into a zone of intense concentration during a round of golf."[16]

Given the relatively small number of junior golfers who ever compile particularly significant professional or amateur records, it would normally not be significant to track the accomplishments of a junior golfer. However, in light of the subsequent success of Tiger Woods as both and amateur and professional, a summary of his junior golf accomplishments is illuminating. Also, much of what he represents today as a professional golfer, businessman, philanthropist, and husband had its foundation in his junior career.

When reviewing Tiger's junior career, it's sometimes difficult to keep in mind that we're talking about a boy, albeit one with exceptionally advanced skills on a golf course. And while he was generally able to compete at a level beyond his age, he was constantly learning and developing his personality under the increasingly intense scrutiny of the sports media. When he was four years old he had his first exposure to some kids cheating in a junior tournament.[17] Tiger observed one of the golfers touching the sand in a bunker (which is punishable by a penalty of two strokes) and not counting those strokes. It was amazing that this four year old was that knowledgeable about the rules of golf, and observant enough to be aware of the violation. More importantly, he told his father, and vowed that he would not cheat even if others cheated. Golf is probably the only popular sport played for money in which competitors actually call penalties on themselves, even if no one else observed the violation.

Golf is also a sport that doesn't depend principally on size and strength. Since Tiger was still small of stature when he began playing competition golf, he sometimes had to overcome feelings of inferiority. An incident occurred at the Junior World Championships in San Diego when Tiger was 12, before he began to grow and fill out physically. He played a six foot tall golfer who drove the first hole. Tiger was intimidated by his size and strength. Earl tells how he counseled Tiger that golf is a game that doesn't depend on size and strength. Tiger eventually defeated that big kid, and vowed to his father that he would not be intimidated again.[18]

In 1989, when he was 13, he competed in the Insurance Youth Golf Classic, a unique tournament in which junior golfers are paired with professionals. Tiger beat eight of the professionals, and paired with future star John Daly and while he eventually lost to Daly on the last few holes, after a brilliant performance, he clearly demonstrated that he could compete on a professional level. He was not yet in high school when he received his first recruiting letter from Stanford University.

In 1990 when he was 14 he won the Optimist International Golf Championship for the fifth time, and he established a record by winning the Junior World Championship six times. As a result of his outstanding record, when he was 15 he was selected as the American Junior Golf Association's Player of the Year, as well as the Southern California Player of the year, and was named to the First Team, on the Rolex Junior All-American list.[19]

The relationship Tiger established with his parents during his junior career was a sensitive balance between trying to please them while learning to compete. Tiger lost the 1990 U.S. Junior Amateur semifinals to Dennis Hillman, and he was severely disappointed. In the car before going home Tiger leaned over, hugged his father and said, "Pop, I love you."[20] Earl also tells of an incident when the 10-year-old Tiger was competing in a junior tournament and faced with a situation that called for the selection of one of a number of possible shots, Tiger chose a shot that seemed odd to Earl. After the round Earl asked him why he decided to use that particular shot. Tiger told him he thought that's what his father wanted him to do. Earl impressed upon Tiger the fact that he was not playing for his father, he was playing for himself, and since he had to live with the consequences of his decisions—in life and on the golf course—he alone could make them. While the media created an image of a happy little boy, unfazed by the outside world, Earl has recounted how Tiger had some recurring nightmares centered around racial bigotry, one where he dreamed he was playing in a tournament in the South and was the target of an assassin. Despite the pressures Tiger might have felt, he continued to excel on the golf course.

He attempted to qualify for the 1991 Nissan Los Angeles Open at South Course at Los Serranos Golf Club in Chino Hills, California. There were two qualifying spots for the 132 players. When he reached the par five 18th hole, his father, who was caddying for Tiger, mistakenly told him he needed a birdie to get one of the two spots. It wouldn't have mattered since Tiger had every intention of going for the green in two when he left the tee. The ball was on a down slope, the lie was bare, and when he swung he didn't catch the ball squarely. The ball landed in the pond in front of the green, thereby dashing any hope of qualifying. The two professionals who did qualify, Mac O'Grady and John Burckle, shot 66. Tiger, after holing out a bogey, shot 69. Several of the professional watching the performance of the 15 year old, were impressed not only with his physical skills, but more importantly his "go for broke" attitude that would characterize his career on the PGA Tour.[21]

On the basis of all the attention he was receiving through the press coverage of his junior record, Tiger was invited to play in the 1992 Los Angeles Open PGA Tournament and while he missed the cut by six shots, he learned a number of valuable lessons about playing on the professional tour. Apparently not everybody playing in the tournament knew about the exploits of Tiger, so when Sandy Lyle was asked about the new phenom, Tiger Woods, he asked if that was a new golf course.[22]

As a consequence of winning the Junior Amateur Tiger was exempt from the local qualifier for the 1992 U.S. Open, and competed in the sectional qualifier held at Lake Merced Country Club in Daly City, California. There were 10 spots for the 77 professionals and exceptional amateurs. Trying to qualify while studying for exams and preparing for his driver's license test took its toll and he missed by four shots. His father noted that this was a good experience for Tiger: since he really had no chance to qualify, there was little pressure on him. But he felt it was a good experience for him to get a feel for the U.S. Open.[23]

By virtue of winning the USGA Junior Amateur Tiger automatically qualified him to compete in the 1992 USGA Amateur. The competition consists of a two-day 36-hole stroke play event from which the 64 low players are allowed to proceed to a match play format. On the first day of the qualifier Tiger had one of his worst rounds as an amateur, not only shooting poorly, but also losing his temper and storming off the course without talking to the media. This was uncharacteristic and ironic since he was certainly not a favorite to qualify; there were plenty of other players in the competition with better records than his. However, it didn't take him long to recover from the bad experience. When asked how long it took him to "cool down" after the round, Tiger was quoted as saying, "Dinner," going on to say he ate 10 tacos. Beyond his emotional recovery, he went out the next day and shot one of his best competitive rounds. He and his father had anticipated needing a score of 69 in order to make the match play rounds. He scored 66, hitting all but two greens in regulation, scoring four birdies, an eagle and 13 pars. Despite the fact that he was eliminated in the second round of match play, this experience once again demonstrated his incomparable ability to rebound after adversity and not allow his emotions to dominate his game.[24]

By 1993 Tiger was finding it difficult to maintain his concentration during rounds, which could have been attributed to the fact that the level of competition in junior golf was not challenging enough anymore. However, he had one more challenge in junior golf and that was to win his third consecutive USGA Junior Championship, to be played at the Waverly Country Club in Portland, Oregon. Tiger made it to the finals, where his opponent was Ryan Armour. Armour was dormie two (meaning a player is two holes up with two holes remaining in the match). This meant Tiger had to win both remaining holes to send the match to extra holes. Tiger birdied the 17th, but hit his second shot on the 18th into a sand bunker some 40 yards from the green. This is one of the most difficult shots in golf under any circumstances, let alone on the final hole of a USGA championship. Tiger hit a spectacular shot to within eight feet of the hole, and sunk the putt. His opponent bogied the hole sending the match to extra holes—in essence, sudden death. Woods defeated his opponent on the first extra hole.[25]

Once again because he had won the USGA Junior Championship in 1993 he was eligible to play in the U.S. Amateur, which was held at the Champions Club in Houston, Texas. Again Tiger was eliminated in the second round of the match play, but it was at this event that he was introduced to Butch Harmon, who would become one of his most trusted teachers and a crucial member of Team Tiger during his transition from amateur to professional golf. Butch was the son of Claude Harmon, the 1948 Masters Champion. After Harmon watched his swing, he told Earl and Tiger that despite his unprecedented accomplishments as a junior golfer, it would be a three-year project to make the complete transition into top flight amateur and professional golf.[26]

The more celebrity Tiger gained, the more he was placed in the spotlight and the more he was subjected to increased scrutiny. Ironically his notoriety resulted in a kind of reverse discrimination. Tiger was offered an honorary membership at Big Canyon Country Club in Newport Beach, California. Earl Woods, very cognizant of the strict rules concerning amateur status in golf, contacted the USGA to find out if Tiger could accept the membership and still remain an amateur. They told Earl that he could, but that Earl should get in touch with the National Collegiate Athletic Association (NCAA), since they might have other stipulations. Earl was somewhat confused about this advice since Tiger was still in high school, but he contacted the NCAA, and at first was told that Tiger couldn't accept the membership and still remain eligible for college golf. Eventually the NCAA granted permission, but this was to be the first in what would become an ongoing series of conflicts and misunderstandings between Team Tiger and the governing body of collegiate sports.[27] Indicative of the difference between golf and other sports, here was Earl Woods assiduously protecting his son's amateur status despite his own strained financial situation. It has been written, albeit cynically, that Earl was hanging on to Tiger's amateur status because there would be a larger payoff down the line. Whatever the reasons, Tiger retained his amateur status. However, it was becoming apparent that even as an amateur the public would demand more from him than his golf game.

Tiger was 14 when the Shoal Creek incident threatened to cancel the 1990 PGA Championship. In a pretournament press conference Hall Thompson, the president of the Shoal Creek Country Club was asked about the lack of any black members in the club. He responded that the club would not be pressured into accepting black members because "that kind of thing isn't done in Alabama." He further exacerbated the situation by stating that the club accepted women, Jews, Lebanese, and Italians. A number of community groups and civil rights groups demonstrated and planned to picket the tournament. However, it wasn't until several of the tournament's corporate sponsors began to feel the financial pressure that anything was done. Eventually, the PGA, and subsequently the USGA, instituted policies that prohibited staging any of their sanctioned tournaments at clubs that discriminated. Suddenly this teenager became the great black hope, and as such the press expected him to have opinions about the racial situation in America. While Tiger was keenly aware of his racial heritage, he didn't want to be the greatest black golfer, he wanted to be the greatest golfer ever.[28] However, as his career evolved he would face more and more pressure to take on the role as spokesman for his race(s), and oppressed minorities in general.

NOTES

1. Earl Woods, *Playing Through* (New York: Harper Collins, 1998), 88.
2. Ibid., 92–93.
3. John Strege, *A Biography of Tiger Woods* (New York: Broadway Books, 1998), 48.
4. Michael Sokolove, "Constructing A Teen Phenom," *New York Times Magazine* November 28, 2004: 80.
5. Ibid., 82.
6. Curt Sampson, *Chasing Tiger* (New York: Atria, 2002), 7.
7. Woods, 99.
8. Ibid., 100.
9. Strege 25.
10. Quoted in ibid., 24.
11. Quoted in ibid., 27.
12. Ibid., 34.
13. Henry Blauvelt, "Woods Finishes With A Good Score, Good Spirits," *USA Today* 21 July 2002, http://www.usatoday.com/sports/golf/2002-07-21-british-woods.htm.
14. Quoted in Strege, 23.
15. Ibid., 35.
16. Quoted in John Andrisani, *Think Like A Tiger* (New York: The Berkley Publishing Group, 2002), 43.
17. Woods, 81–82.
18. Ibid., 91–92.
19. Edwards, 27.
20. Quoted in Strege, 33.
21. Ibid., 41.

22. Ibid., 50.
23. Ibid., 54.
24. Ibid., 56–57.
25. Ibid., 59.
26. Ibid., 61.
27. Ibid., 53.
28. Ibid., 39.

Tiger poses for a photograph with his father and mother, Earl and Kultida Woods, on September 22, 1990. Courtesy of Getty Images.

Nineteen-year-old Tiger Woods with the U.S. Amateur Championship Trophy at the TPC at Sawgrass in Ponte Vedra Beach, Florida in 1994. Courtesy of Getty Images.

Tiger Woods in 1999. Courtesy of Photofest.

Tiger at "Battle at Bighorn," a made-for-television prime-time event at the Bighorn Golf Club in Palm Desert, California, 2001. Courtesy of Photofest.

Tiger defending his title in 2001 (British) Open
Championship at Royal Lytham & St. Anne's Golf
Club in England. Courtesy of Photofest.

Tiger teeing off at Disney Golf Classic in Lake Buena
Vista, Florida, 2002. Courtesy of Photofest.

Tiger Woods and Elin Nordegren arrive at the 35th
Ryder Cup Matches Gala Dinner at the Fox Theatre
on September 15, 2004 in Detroit, Michigan.
Courtesy of Getty Images.

Chapter 4

PIONEERS

In 1995 Tiger Woods received an award from a little known nine-hole golf course in Indianapolis, Indiana. Douglass Park Golf Course was one of the prominent stops on what represented a segregation-induced black golfers' tour until the PGA of America eliminated its racial exclusion from its constitution in 1961. A month later he played in his first Masters Tournament, as reigning U.S. Amateur Champion. Commenting later on the significance of his predecessors, he said, "I have a great deal of reverence for the Masters tradition, especially since my victory in 1997, but I must admit, the first time I drove down Magnolia Lane I was not thinking about Bobby Jones or all the Masters stood for: I was thinking about all the great African American players who never got a chance to play there. That I was able to win there, I believe, brought a little bit of vindication."[1]

It is important to trace a brief history of the game because part of the intense interest in Tiger Woods is the fact that he is of mixed race playing a game that throughout most of its history excluded minorities. In order to fully appreciate the accomplishments of Tiger Woods, it's significant that the reader should understand the tremendous obstacles that have prevented people of color from establishing a presence in the sport of golf, both in the professional ranks, and in most of the private clubs and courses throughout America. And it's not without some irony, given the history of the game, that there's ample evidence that the first American-born professional golfer was an African American.

DEVELOPMENT OF THE GAME

No other sport has stratified social classes like the game of golf. The game of golf was first played by shepherds in Scotland who probably observed Roman soldiers playing a game called *paganica*,[2] which was played with a bent stick hitting a leather ball stuffed with feathers. So the game was not originally a gentleman's game. By 1457 the game was popular enough to be banned by the parliament of James II because it took too much time away from archery practice. Between the lifting of the ban in 1502 and the mid-nineteenth century, the game was played by British gentleman amateurs on courses throughout the country and wherever the empire spread.

The first generation of professional golfers, not unlike boxers, used the game to raise themselves up out of poverty. The golfers we remember are not the gentleman amateurs who played the game in Stuart Scotland. Between 1830 and 1860 three Scots pioneered the sport: Old Tom Morris, Alan Robertson, and Old Tom's son Tom, Jr. who dropped dead of grief at 24, hours after his wife died in childbirth. The British Open Championship—or, as the British prefer the Open Championship—was first played in 1860.

In 1877, Harry Vardon's family was evicted from their shanty to make way for the Royal Jersey Golf Club. Vardon would become the first golfer to gain an international reputation, and as such, would be the precursor to Tiger Woods. It should be pointed out that he was typical of the golf professionals of the day and was probably the first who was able to capitalize on his playing prowess financially beyond the prize money. At this time golf was a game for gentleman-amateurs: professionals were not well respected by civilized society, were largely uneducated, spoke with thick regional accents and lacked social graces. Their main role was to make and repair golf clubs, tend to the care of the golf course and teach the members how to improve their games. If they were good enough they would occasionally compete in tournaments. When they did, they were rarely allowed to even change their shoes in the clubhouses, let alone eat lunch in the club dining room.[3]

Bobby Jones was the true embodiment of the ideal of amateurism when he won the so-called Grand Slam of golf in 1930: the U.S. Open, the U.S. Amateur, the British Amateur, and the British Open. Jones would later gain fame as the founder of the Masters Golf Tournament and the world-renowned Augusta National Golf Course. On display at the USGA headquarters in Far Hills, New Jersey are the four medals he received, in lieu of the cash prize he would have been awarded for winning the two

Open Championships. Jones, a lawyer, never turned professional and to this day represents to some the quintessential amateur. Of course it must be pointed out that in 1930 there was little money to be made in golf by today's standards. The connection between the sport and commerce had not yet been made. Most significantly, the media was in its infancy and had a limited ability to create much mass interest in the game.

In comparison to other sports, the game of golf does not on the surface generate much passion. It is one of the only sports in which spectators must remain completely quiet during play. It is the only sport in which the match takes place simultaneously over a 20-acre tract of land. Most competitors themselves exhibit little show of emotion. So how has this sport managed to periodically capture the imagination of the sports public and gain large audiences and mass media coverage? Every so often there emerges a player who, by virtue of their personality and flair, captures the public's imagination. Vardon and Jones were early examples this phenomenon; Tiger Woods is the latest incarnation. Players with this kind of appeal transform the game from a slow, plodding test of endurance to a dramatic performance. We relate to golfers because they play a sport which is conducted in open space with no walls or barriers between the spectator and the player. They wear clothes that roughly approximate our own—no helmets, funny socks, or shorts. It's the sport that most closely reflects the style of the period and place it is played, and while the game began in Britain, it adapted well to America.

The South Carolina Golf Course was established in 1876 in Charleston, South Carolina, and is arguably the first golf club in America.[4] However, it wasn't until the 1890s that golf was played in earnest in the U.S. Willie Dunn, a Scotsman, came to America in 1891 and built the first incorporated,[5] formally designed golf course at Shinnecock Hills, on Long Island. The game was imported from Britain by wealthy American businessmen who had the reason and means to travel to Europe. While the game was played principally by the wealthy, African Americans played an important role in the early development of the game in America.

AFRICAN AMERICANS AND GOLF

African Americans have been involved with the game of golf since it was played in America. While that connection was almost exclusively as caddies, they inevitably developed the skills to play the game. However, it would be a long time before blacks would be able to play the game legitimately on a golf course. By the early 1920s, there was a golf boom that fueled an unending need for caddies at both private and public courses.

Traditionally clubs allowed caddies to play on the one day a week when the courses were closed to members for maintenance, and it appears that caddy masters were fairly color blind when it came to letting the caddies play. Consequently, many young black teenagers were able to play on courses that would not allow them as members, even if they could afford it. While the caddies did earn some playing privileges, they were still shown little respect. A former black caddy at Augusta liked to tell the story of a black caddy who grumbled when the great emancipator's son tipped him a dime after a round. "Northern gentlemen usually give me a quarter," he said. Lincoln glared, "Didn't my father do enough for you people already?" "I don't know, I never caddied for your father," was his response.[6]

Despite the limited opportunity to play golf, enough black people developed an interest in the game so that a number of black-owned golf clubs were founded as early as the 1920s. Although these were not posh layouts and many were poorly maintained nine-hole courses, they did provide a way for interested black people to play golf regularly. One such club was Shady Rest Golf Club in Westfield (now Scotch Plains), New Jersey, established in 1921. The members consisted of "prosperous Negro merchants, lawyers, doctors, Pullman porters, waiters and janitors".[7]

Shady Rest

Shady Rest started out as the Westfield Country Club which was established in 1900 and featured a nine-hole golf course north of the Westfield train line on Jerusalem Road in Scotch Plains, New Jersey. On either side of the club was an African American community of small houses and the residents would routinely cut across the golf course to get to the train line or to socialize. Over a period of years a "right of travel" evolved which later affected the legal rights of the all-white private club, and in 1921 when the Westfield Country Club considered plans to expand the course to 18 holes, but this legal condition undoubtedly affected their decision to sell the club and merge with the Cranford Golf Club to form the Echo Lake Country Club in Springfield. The former Westfield club was mortgaged to the Progressive Realty Company, created by a group of prominent African Americans and became the Shady Rest Golf and Country Club, considered to be the first African American golf and country club in America.[8]

There were other black-owned and/or operated golf courses before and during this period, but none of them had combined golf with the club house, restaurant, lockers, tennis courts, horseback riding, skeet shooting, croquet and social activities that were available at Shady Rest and generally associated with country clubs of the era. Shady Rest was run by and for blacks, and became an important social and economic institution in the local community and the New York metropolitan area.

In 1925 a fight for control of Shady Rest erupted over mismanagement of the club's finances between forces representing a New York contingent headed by Henry Parker and a local group from New Jersey. The local group managed to vote out the New York slate of club officers, but the New York group was reinstated after the election was challenged in the courts. Following this controversy it was rumored that Parker and another New York member, John E. Nail, left Shady Rest along with money collected to pay off the mortgage, leaving the club in substantial debt.[9] It was at this point that William Willis Sr. assumed control of Shady Rest.

William Willis Sr. ran Shady Rest for the remainder of its history. In many ways he represents the struggle of African Americans entering the mainstream of middle-class America. He served in the Army during World War I and became a supply sergeant. Upon returning the United State she started a taxi cab company and began dealing in real estate in the Scotch Plains area. However, sometime in the early 1930s, because of the rising tax levies, Shady Rest was forced to change ownership and became the property of the township of Scotch Plains.[10] Through an informal agreement, the municipality committed to retain the club for the African American community, and Willis agreed to continue running it.

In 1963, the gentlemen's handshake between William Willis Sr. and the township of Scotch Plains came to an end. Shady Rest became the Scotch Hills Country Club and was opened to the public. While the end of Shady Rest is linked to the rise of integration in public facilities in the 1960s, there is ambivalence over the inevitable deterioration of African American institutions.

Shady Rest provided a forum for some of the most prominent African Americans of the period, from all spheres of influence. Because of its proximity to New York, many famous musicians performed regularly at the club. Ella Fitzgerald, Count Basie, and Duke Ellington all made appearances at Shady Rest. The late Althea Gibson learned to play tennis and later golf at Shady Rest. On Memorial Day 1923 over five hundred automobiles from all over the Northeast jammed the parking lot at Shady Rest as an overflow crowd gathered to hear W.E.B. DuBois, the distinguished activist-scholar, lecture.[11] The club boasted a membership of working-class and professional men and women and their families, and provided an atmosphere of civility and belonging in what could otherwise be a hostile and unfriendly world.

The story of Shady Rest represents a symbol of black achievement during a period when African Americans were suffering even more than Depression-era white Americans. The club offered the evolving black middle class a social and economic institution with access to activities not associated with a minority community.

John Shippen

One person intimately connected to the Shady Rest Country Club, and relatively overlooked until recently, was John M. Shippen. During the ABC telecasts of the 1981 and 1984 U.S. Open, Jim Thorpe was referred to as the first Native American to lead the U.S. Open in its history. Jerry Izenberg, a syndicated sports columnist for the New Jersey's Newark *Star Ledger*, wrote a column challenging that statement and telling the story of John Shippen.[12]

Shippen was born in December 1878 in the Washington, D.C. area and his family came to Long Island in 1888. Shippen's father was a Presbyterian minister, and his ministry was with the Shinnecock Indian Reservation. Shippen recounted that by 1893 he was caddying and playing golf at Shinnecock, and that he was party to a number of matches with the members of Shinnecock (who would put up $50 purses). He said he played Shinnecock golf professional R.B. Wilson four times and beat him three times.[13]

Shippen, then 18 years old, competed in the 1896 Open along with Shinnecock Indian and fellow caddie Oscar Bunn, and a racial incident occurred that has led to some question and controversy concerning the racial identity of John Shippen. Shippen, then an assistant to Willie Dunn, the professional at Shinnecock Hills, almost didn't compete because a group of mostly foreign-born professionals and amateurs threatened to boycott the tournament if Shippen and Oscar Bunn were allowed to play. Theodore Havemeyer, the president of the newly formed United States Golf Association, is reported to have informed the disgruntled golfers that the tournament would be run even if Shippen and Bunn were the only two competitors. According to this story, the other golfers relented and they competed in the tournament with Shippen and Bunn. Different versions of the story have survived. One has Havemeyer telling the other players that Shippen was not a Negro, but an Indian, and this supposedly quelled the uprising. This version of the story is less plausible in light of a reference in a now-extinct British publication of the period, *The Golfer*, in which there is a reference to "John Shippen, a sixteen-year-old coloured caddie attached to the Shinnecock Hills course."[14]

This incident has relevance here since we are examining the life of certainly the most prominent golfer of mixed race in the history of the sport of golf, and it is important to point out that as far back as the turn of the century there were overt examples of discrimination based on race in the sport of golf. And, historically, the fact that an African American was competing for the national golf championship of the United States in 1896 is significant.[15]

To the extent that African American's or anyone's race in America can be definitively ascertained, it seems clear that John Shippen was the child of predominantly African American parents. Two of Shippen's daughters contributed their recollections to a book written by Paul E. Sluby in which they say, "Milton Winfield Lee, our great grandfather, was the first of our Lee lineage who was of Shinnecock heritage."[16] And Shippen himself identified his father was a "Negro" and his mother was a Shinnecock Indian.[17] The question of Shippen's race has taken on increased significance since the fight for civil rights in the '50s and '60s, and particularly with the arrival of African American professionals on the PGA Tour.

There are several factors which have clouded the ethnic origins of John Shippen over the years. The principal point of confusion is the fact that John Shippen married a Shinnecock Indian woman, so his children were also of mixed ethnic background. Among the Shinnecock tribe there are many examples of intermarriage with African Americans. Finally, it was apparently not always easy for disinterested Shinnecock members to distinguish the ethnic origins of the help. From photographs of Shippen it is evident that his ethnic origins could have been mistaken. The fact that there is a debate about the ethnic heritage of John Shippen is a significant indication of the status of American blacks during this period. Furthermore, it is interesting to speculate about the controversy surrounding whether or not Shippen and Bunn would be allowed to play in the 1896 Open. As the name implies, the tournament was open to both professionals and amateurs. Given the humble station of virtually all golf professionals of the period, it is unlikely they would have cared who competed in the tournament. It is much more likely that the amateur golfers would have taken exception to these ethnic outcasts being included. In the final standings Shippen tied for fifth place in the Open competition with H.J. Whigham of Onwentsia, the player who had won the amateur competition the day before.

Shippen left caddying, and took his first professional job teaching golf to the wealthy Cromwell family of Bernardsville, New Jersey.[18] For the next two years Shippen served as the golf professional at the Maidstone Golf Club in East Hampton. After working at several Metropolitan area clubs in New Jersey (Spring Lake) and Brooklyn (Marine and Field Club—which became the Dyke Beach Club), Shippen returned to Maidstone where he worked from 1902 until 1913. He was next employed for a year as a private professional for steel tycoon Henry Clay Frick. In 1916 Shippen returned to Shinnecock to serve as greenskeeper for two years, after which he served in a similar capacity for the National Golf Links, which is adjacent to Shinnecock. He then moved to Washington, D.C., left golf and worked for several years for the Department of Public Grounds. Shippen's family was originally from Washington and consequently he had family there which precipitated his return.

Shippen went back to golf and worked for the National Capital Golf Club, a black club in Maryland. In 1932 he went to back to New Jersey and became the professional at the Shady Rest Country Club. He would work there until he died in 1968.

During the time Shippen was playing competitive golf, the only significant tournament in which professionals could compete was the U.S. Open Championship. So it is worth listing his accomplishments in that prestigious event, despite the many obstacles that faced an African American golfer during this period:

1896: July 18 (36 holes played the same day), Shinnecock Hills. 78–81 = 159. Tied for 5th. Affiliated: Shinnecock Hills.
1899: September 14–15, Baltimore Country Club. 86–88–88–88 = 350. 27th. Affiliated: Aronimink (Philadelphia).
1900: October 4–5, Chicago Country Club. 181–89–83 = 353. Tie 25th. Affiliated: Marine & Field (Brooklyn).
1902: October 10–11, Garden City Golf Course. 79–82–76–81 = 318. Tie 5th. Affiliated: New York
1913: September 16, 17, 18, 19, The Country Club, Brookline, MA.[19] (165 qualifying score) 81–73–87–87 = 328. Tie 41st. Affiliated: Maidstone Golf Club (Long Island).

Apparently during this period, the USGA only listed the players who completed the competition and handed in a scorecard, because the records indicate more entries than final scores listed. So it is possible that Shippen participated in more Opens but did not finish. However, considering his financial situation, it is unlikely he competed in many other tournaments. During this period there were few other opportunities to compete since there was not a golf tour.

The Professional Golfers Association was not formed until 1916, so technically there was no such thing as a golf professional when Shippen played the game competitively, so he would never become a member of the PGA. He worked in the game for over 70 years, and fulfilled the responsibilities of what a golf professional did during the period—keeping the course in good playing condition; supplying and repairing equipment; teaching; serving as starter and scorekeeper for tournaments, and occasionally playing for prize money—it is safe to refer to Shippen as the first American-born golf professional.[20] By the time Shippen took the job at Shady Rest he was 54 and his competitive golfing days were over.

Shady Rest was not the first, nor the only, golf club exclusively for African Americans. At about the same time, black golfers in Washington, D.C., found it increasingly difficult to gain access to courses in the area. Because of the federal government's growing sensitivity to equal rights, there were probably more emerging middle-class blacks in Washington, D.C., than any other area of the country. Blacks there had better jobs, more leisure time, and access to municipal courses, so this area produced the most African American golfers. In 1938 a coalition of men and women black golfers petitioned the Secretary of State, Harold Ickes, to desegregate Washington's public golf courses, and one of the results was the building of Langston Course in 1939.[21]

So strong was their interest in the game that several of these Washingtonians rented summer cottages in Stow, Massachusetts, where Dr. John Ritt Randall, a wealthy, Harvard-educated doctor had constructed a golf course on his family's estate.[22] The Mapledale Country Club would play a significant role in the development of black golf in America.

Other early black-owned clubs were: Sunset Hills Country Club, Kankakee, Illinois; Lincoln Country Club of Atlanta, Georgia; Freeway Golf Course in Sicklerville, and the Asbury Park Course in New Jersey. As more golf courses became available to blacks throughout the country, the desire for competition increased.

In 1925, the first National Colored Golf Championship was held at Shady Rest. The winner of the inaugural event was Harry Jackson and the runner-up was John Shippen, both from the Washington, D.C. area.[23] This championship was organized by a group formed earlier that the year in Washington, D.C., called the United States Colored Golfers Association. B.C. Gordon, president of Shady Rest, was elected the president of the association. Two years later the group was renamed the United Golfers Association, an organization that served as the governing body of black golf until desegregation opened up many public courses to blacks in the mid '60s.

The United Golfers Association

By 1926 there were enough black clubs across the country so that Robert Hawkins, a resident of Stow, was able to invite the known black clubs throughout the United States to a tournament at his Mapledale course. On Labor Day weekend, 1926, 35 black golfers came to play the 72-hole medal (stroke) tournament. The winner of the professional division was paid $100; the amateurs received medals. The men's and women's winners of that inaugural event were Harry Jackson of Washington, D.C. and Marie Thompson of Chicago. John Shippen finished fourth and won $25.[24]

The UGA consisted of regional organizations of black golfers, such as the Eastern Golfers Association, which would periodically stage competitions for individual members and interclub matches. The UGA coordinated the scheduling of these events, and sponsored an annual national championship held at various black clubs throughout the country. These events usually consisted of an amateur competition and an open competition. As the number of tournaments increased, the prize money available also increased, thus luring more and more black golfers to play golf professionally. The first president of the UGA was Dr. George W. Adams, Jr., who was also founding member of the Royal Golf Club of Washington, D.C., which led to a proliferation of local clubs organized into regions across the country. He was reelected in 1929.[25] Two important women in the history of the UGA were Ms. Paris Brown and Ms. Anna M. Robinson, who served as historian and tour director.

There is ample evidence that African American women took a more active role in establishing opportunities to play golf than their Caucasian counterparts. The first formally organized women's golf club, the Wake-Robin Golf Club, was started in Washington, D.C. in 1937. It should be noted that this club was not an auxiliary of a men's club. Several months later, the Chicago Women's Golf Club was established. It is important to explain that these clubs did not own golf courses. They usually had access to a public course on certain days and times when they were permitted to play their tournaments.[26]

Black women faced all the same obstacles presented to the men, yet the UGA was able to nurture several outstanding women golfers, some of whom went on to compete in the Ladies Professional Golf Association and distinguish themselves. Ann Gregory of Gary, Indiana became the first black woman to compete in a USGA Amateur Championship in 1957 at Meridian Hills Country Club in Indianapolis, followed by Eoline Thorton of Long Beach, California in 1958. Althea Gibson, who played golf at Shady Rest, after having a highly visible championship tennis career, took up golf and became the first black woman to compete on the LPGA circuit in 1967. Renee Powell, whose father William built and operated the Clearview Country Club in Canton, Ohio, had a successful college career at both Ohio State and Ohio Universities. She played for several years in the late '60s on the women's tour.

Throughout the years when black professional golfers were unable to compete on the PGA Tour, the UGA served as the only opportunity for these golfers to showcase their abilities and, for some, to earn at least a modest living playing golf. It also represented a social network for middle-class blacks who were otherwise excluded from the social institutions associated with the game.

While the UGA provided an opportunity for black club pros and amateurs to test their skills against other club players, it had little success in promoting black golfers into the major white golf establishment. The United States Golf Association didn't reserve any places in its annual championship for members of the UGA—as the United States Lawn Tennis Association did for the American Tennis Association (the UGA's tennis counterpart). There was very little interaction between the USGA and the UGA. It wasn't until 1959 that any USGA championship was won by a black person, when Bill Wright won the Public Links Championship. Subsequently, Charles Duhon won the 1982 USGA Senior Amateur Championship in 1982. After winning consecutive USGA Junior Championships, Tiger Woods became the first amateur golfer ever to win three consecutive USGA Amateur Championships in 1994, 1995, and 1996.

While many accomplished black golfers were spawned by the activities of the UGA, because of the limited national media coverage of their tournaments, many went unheralded. Robert "Pat" Ball from Chicago won UGA professional titles in 1927, 1929, 1934, and 1941. Howard "Butch" Wheeler, who was Bobby Jones' favorite caddie at the Brookhaven Country Club, was known for his long drives. He was the UGA professional champion five times between 1933 and 1958.[27]

The military service and black colleges were two other avenues for the development of black golfers. For some, the army offered the only opportunity to play on 18-hole courses which approached championship caliber. Pvt. Calvin Searles (who subsequently died in WWII) played in the 1944 Tam O'Shanter All American event. This was the only mainstream tournament that allowed blacks to compete during the war years. The only black college with its own course was Tuskegee Institute, a three-hole course built in 1920 which was eventually expanded to nine holes in the '30s. Tuskegee sponsored the first black intercollegiate tournament in 1938, and they established a National Intercollegiate event in 1940.[28]

The Fight for Equality

African Americans were also making efforts to increase access to public courses. The opportunity to play these courses offered the only real chance to improve the overall skills of the growing number of black golfers. In several cases around the country blacks were suing to gain either access or increased access to public facilities, along with other civil rights efforts of the period.

A black dentist, Dr. P.O. Sweeny, sued the Louisville (Kentucky) Parks Department in 1947 for the right to play unrestricted on the public courses there. The decision ruled, in essence, that the courts could not enforce social equality and the suit was dismissed.[29] Other lower court cases yielded similar results or, in some cases, modified rules for access. There followed a host of court cases which eventually led the Supreme Court, in 1955, to reaffirm its rejection of "separate but equal" accommodations for public golf and recreational facilities. In the relevant case, the Court vacated a ruling by a lower court that allowed Atlanta to legally segregate blacks and whites if the facilities were of equal quality. However, the ruling did not immediately open up public golf courses to black golfers.

The struggle of black professionals took to the courts as well as the national media. In 1948, Ted Rhodes, Bill Spiller and Gunter Madison, accomplished black golfers, forced the PGA to rethink its exclusionary rule. These golfers brought suit against the PGA for discrimination when they were not allowed to compete in the Richmond Open in Richmond, California.[30] The case was settled out of court in September 1948 when "the PGA, through attorney Dana Murdock, declared ... that it would not discriminate or refuse tournament playing privileges to anyone because of color."[31] However, discrimination on the professional tour continued.

At the 1952 San Diego Open, Joe Louis, himself an accomplished amateur golfer, was invited by a local Chevrolet sponsor to participate in the tournament.[32] A PGA committee notified Louis that he was banned from participation. While the PGA constitution prohibited non-Caucasians from membership in the PGA, Louis had been invited, according to the rules, by the local sponsor as one of five amateur golfers allowed, without the need for qualification.

Horton Smith, PGA president, eventually polled the members of the executive committee to gain an exemption for Louis to compete. The

PGA added a clause to their by-laws that allowed one PGA-approved "Negro" amateur (under 5 handicap) and one PGA-approved "Negro" professional of "recognized standing and ability" to be designated by local sponsors to compete in PGA events. Despite the national attention generated by the San Diego Open racial controversy, it would be for nine years before the PGA would officially rescind its "Caucasian only" clause.

Charlie Sifford was the most prominent black professional golfer between 1945 and 1970, and the black golf professional most discriminated against. Aside from John Shippen, he accomplished the most "black firsts" in golf. After dominating the annual UGA professional championship, winning a record five in a row between 1952 and 1956, he became the first black player to win a significant title in a predominantly white event, the Long Beach (California) Open in 1957.[33] While Pete Brown, another early black professional, helped pave the way for other black professionals, as the first black pro to win a PGA tournament (the 1964 Waco Turner Open) Sifford became the first black player to win a major PGA event, the 1969 Los Angeles Open. Sifford began playing golf as a caddie in Greensboro, N.C., where he won several local events. He then moved north to Philadelphia where he worked as a teaching professional.

In 1960, after receiving a letter of protest from Charlie Sifford, the attorney general of California, Stanley Mosk, announced "we intend to take every step available to us, both in and out of the courts, to force the PGA either to eliminate this obnoxious restriction or to cease all activity of any kind within our state."[34] Eventually the executive committee of the PGA voted to eliminate racial restriction for membership. The full membership of the PGA ratified the committee's decision in November 1961.[35] Charlie Sifford eventually received his Class "A" PGA card in 1964.

In the 1969 Greater Greensboro Open, Sifford missed an opportunity to qualify for the 1970 Masters, the most exclusive invitational event on the professional golf tour, when he encountered heckling from several white spectators. Coming into the tournament, Sifford was in tenth position on a point list to qualify for the Masters; the top six would qualify. Four white men began heckling Sifford, prompting this comment from George Walsh, the tournament supervisor: "I followed them for four holes. I told them we wanted everybody to have a good time and asked them to stop it. But they didn't and I had the deputy detain them until a state patrolman arrived to arrest them.[36]

The black golfer who played the most prominent public role in bringing black golf to the attention of the sporting world was Lee Elder. After competing mainly in UGA tournaments, Elder earned his PGA card in 1967.[37]

Elder is best known as the first black golfer to compete in the Masters. This tournament, played on Augusta National Golf Course in Augusta, Georgia, is the ultimate symbol of the exclusivity of golf. The club has one of the most restricted memberships among all private clubs, and over the years, the tournament represented the inability of African American golfers to gain equality in major tournament golf. Unlike most PGA events, only invited golfers are allowed to compete in the Masters. Most other PGA events were open to any golfer who finished the previous year in the top 60 money winners on the tour or was able to qualify for any remaining open spots. No black had ever been invited to the Masters.

Throughout the early 70s, Elder was the focal point of an effort to force the officials who ran the Masters to establish permanent criteria for a golfer to obtain an invitation to the tournament. In 1971 the Masters changed earlier policies that invited players on the basis of a complicated point system and by ballot of former Masters champions. The new policy granted an invitation to anyone who won a PGA tournament in the year prior to the Masters.[38] Finally, in 1974, Elder won the Monsanto Open which qualified him to compete in the 1975 Masters.

The most successful black golfer before Tiger Woods was Calvin Peete. Ironically, Peete did not come to golf by a traditional route. Born in Detroit in 1943, Peete was one of nineteen children. His family moved South after the war and he grew up in Pahokee, Florida. He made a living selling trinkets to migrant fruit pickers up and down the East coast. On one trip to northern most stop in Rochester, New York, friends tricked him into playing golf. He was 23 years old.[39]

In addition to his late start, he was further hampered by a left arm he could not straighten out due to a childhood injury. But he persevered. By 1971 he had turned professional, and earned his tour card by 1975. Since then, he accomplished what no black golfer had before. He won his first PGA tournament in 1978, the Greater Milwaukee Open, coincidentally Tiger's first professional win, and became the first black pro to earn $100,000. By the end of 1984, Peete was won the most tournaments on the PGA Tour over the preceding four years.[40]

In 1982 he became the first black multiple winner, capturing the Greater Milwaukee Open (for the second time), the Anheuser-Busch Classic, the BC Open and the Pensacola Open, and had his best finish of an African American golf professional in a Grand Slam event, placing third in the 1982 PGA Championship.

The accomplishments of early black golf professionals certainly were instrumental in creating interest in the game among the African American community, and making the career of Tiger Woods possible.

Undoubtedly the emergence of Tiger Woods as a dominant figure in professional golf has further helped popularize the sport in the minority communities, in particular the proliferation of minority junior golf programs. The organizations that control the sport of golf also have clearly made a commitment to eliminate discrimination. However, despite the phenomenal spotlight which the success of Woods has shown on black golfers, and all the policy changes with respect to host clubs for PGA and USGA events, there has been limited progress in the increase of number of minority members at local private clubs. While the historic legacy of "separate but equal" continues to manifest itself in at the recreational level, the amateur and professional career of Tiger Woods dispelled any question of the ability of minorities to excel at the game.

NOTES

1. Quoted in Pete McDaniel, *Uneven Lies: The Heroic Story of African-Americans in Golf* (Greenwich, Connecticut: American Golfer, 2000), 9.

2. "Golf," *The World Book Encyclopedia* (Chicago: Field Enterprises Educational Corporation, 1976), 255.

3. Mark Frost, *The Greatest Game Ever Played* (New York: Hyperion, 2002), 12.

4. Calvin Sinnette, *Forbidden Fairways* (Chelsea, Minn.: Sleeping Bear Publications, 1998), 4.

5. Tom Flaherty, *The U.S. Open (1895–1965): Complete Story of the United States Golf Championship* (New York: E.P. Dutton & Co., 1966), 18.

6. Flaherty, 39.

7. Social Cataclysm, "Only Golf Course in U.S. is Thriving in Suburban Jersey," *New York Sun*, 11 July 1922: 22.

8. *A Place For Us: The Story of Shady Rest and America's First Golf Professional* dir. Larry Londino, WNET Channel 13, 19 December1996.

9. Lester A. Walton, "Shady Rest Club Ends Big Fight in Jersey Courts," *Pittsburgh Courier*, 18 July 1925: 9.

10. William Willis Jr., personal interview, 14 October 1991.

11. "Thousands Motored Out to Shady Rest Country Club Decoration Day," *Amsterdam News*, 6 June 1923: 5.

12. Jerry Izenberg, *Sunday Star Ledger*, 17 June 1984: 28.

13. Frank Strafaci, "Forgotten Pioneer Professional," *Golfing Magazine*, March 1957: 11.

14. *The Golfer*, 5 August 1896: 109.

15. In the course of my own research for a documentary about John Shippen and the place where he spent most of his professional golfing life, the Shady Rest Country Club, I was able to meet and interview a number of people who knew him and caddied for him. I met his grandson, Hanno Shippen Smith.

16. Paul E. Sluby, Sr., *The Family Recollections of Beulah A. Shippen and Mabel S.(Shippen) Hatcher,* (Self-published, 1994), 43.

17. Strafaci, 12.

18. Ibid., 12.

19. This is the Open that established American golf. Francis Quimet, a twenty-one-year-old former caddy and amateur who had never won any national championship, staged a heroic quest and defeated British professionals Harry Vardon and Ted Ray in a dramatic 18-hole playoff at the Country Club in Brookline, Massachusetts. The story of Quimet's quixotic journey is brilliantly chronicled in Mark Frost's 2002 book, *The Greatest Game Ever Played.*

20. Lawrence Londino, "Shady Rest: Itself a Strong Ship," *Golf Journal* Spring, 1996: 17.

21. Ron Lux, "Golf Pioneers by Necessity," *Golf Leisure,* fall 1989.

22. Richard Porter Preiss, *Mashies At Mapledale: A Black Country Club in Massachusetts During the 1920's.* Paper presented at North American Society for Sport History Convention, Vancouver, British Columbia, Canada, 24–25 May 1986: 1.

23. *Baltimore Afro-American,* 18 July 1925: 6.

24. Preiss, 7.

25. Guilford Jones, "Past Greats," *Black Sports,* July 1973: 65–66.

26. Calvin Sinnette, 99–100.

27. Arthur Ashe, Jr., *A Hard Road to Glory: 1919 to 1945* (Warner Books, 1988), 67.

28. A.S. Young, *Negro First in Sports* (Chicago: Johnson Publishing Company, 1963), 164.

29. Ibid., 166.

30. Bill Mardo, "2 Negros Golfers Sue PGA for $250,000," *Daily Worker,* 16 January 1948: Back page.

31. "Will Not Bar Negroes: P.G.A. Revises Attitude, Suit by 3 Pros Dismissed," *New York Times,* 22 September 1948: 45.

32. "P.G.A. Committee Votes to Ease Tourney Ban on Negro Players," *New York Times,* 14 January 1952: 25.

33. Young, 163.

34. "Will Not Bar Negroes," *New York Times,* 23 November 1960: 163.

35. "P.G.A. Will Shift '62 Tourney Site," *New York Times,* 18 May 1961: 45.

36. Lincoln A. Werden, "4 Men Removed After Heckling Sifford, Negro Golf Pro, in Greensboro Open," *New York Times,* 5 April 1969: 35.

37. "Elder Denies He Made Charge of Race Bias in Pensacola Golf," *New York Times,* 6 June 1969: 49.

38. "Masters Policy Change Seen As Aid to Blacks," *New York Times,* 13 June 1971: Sec V, 5.

39. Ashe, 154.

40. Ibid., 157.

Chapter 5

THE RECORD

AMATEUR CAREER

While Tiger Woods is statistically the most successful professional golfer in the shortest period of time, his amateur record—in particular his three consecutive victories in the U.S. Amateur Championship—was a definitive forecast of what was to come. Even though today the public's attention is clearly focused on the professional game, the early popularity of the game originated with amateur golf. The fabulous amateur career of Tiger Woods helped rejuvenate the public's interest in the amateur game, and in order to fully appreciate the career of Tiger Woods we should first understand something about the origins of the game, and the role amateur golf played in that history.

The USGA is the preeminent governing body of golf in America. The championships conducted by them are important because they represent the national championships of the United States. Considering the lofty reputation of American golf in the world, the USGA Amateur Championship is arguably the most important amateur title to win. And while American culture values monetary accomplishment, there has always been prestige attached to people who play only for the title and a medal, not cash. Call it romantic, but there's something to be said for the golfer who is not sullied by the taint of commercialism, retains his amateur purity, and plays the game just for the joy of competition. While the game was first played in Scotland by the peasant classes, by the time it came to America, only people of means were able to embrace the game.

It was played recreationally by people who didn't have to depend on golf to earn a living.

By 1894 there was enough interest in the game of golf in America to justify two so-called national amateur championships. In an effort to create a governing body that would oversee one championship, Charles MacDonald, prominent businessman and amateur golfer, and who himself was runner up in both championships, called for a meeting of the representatives from prominent existing golf clubs. The result of that meeting was the establishment of The Amateur Golf Association of the United States on December 22, 1894. Reflecting the increased number of non-amateur golfers, the name was soon changed to the United States Golf Association. There were five charter member clubs: Newport Golf Club, Shinnecock Hills Golf Club, The Country Club (Brookline, Massachussetts), St. Andrew's Golf Club (Yonkers, New York), and Chicago Golf Club.[1]

The first USGA Amateur Championship was held at the Newport Golf Club in Rhode Island, a nine-hole course, in October, 1895. The original date was changed because of a conflict with the America's Cup Yacht races, which gives some indication of who the competitors and interested spectators would be. It should be pointed out that the Open competition was held the same week, but was merely an afterthought of the main event which was the Amateur. Author Mark Frost explains the attitude of most Americans toward golf's national championship:

> . . . the USGA's National Amateur Championship received the lion's share of attention America paid to the sport of golf during the first decade of the twentieth century. It was the main event played by the sport's founding fathers, upper-crust captains of industry. They and their social equals who could afford the time–consuming sport still looked slightly askance at the U.S. Open as a Masonic cloister of lower-class, foreign-born professionals, gathering like an annual tradesman's guild convention. The truth was neither the press nor the public could get that worked up about a bunch of hard-faced immigrant Scotsmen wrestling amongst themselves not simply for honor, but for a negligible pile of cash.[2]

In fact there was relatively little interest in the sport at this point since it was remote from the majority of American's daily lives. It wasn't until the 1913 U.S. Open was won by a scrappy former caddie named Francis Ouimet that the general public began to follow golf. Ouimet played the role of David to Scotland's dual Goliaths, in the persons of Tom Vardon and Ted Ray, seasoned, veteran professionals who dominated the sport. It was during this upset that the British-dominated sport finally caught the attention of the American public, who were rooting for one of their own.

If Francis Ouimet put the sport of golf on the map in America, it was an unassuming young man from Atlanta, Georgia, Robert "Bobby" Tyre Jones Jr., who kept it there. While there are many parallels between the junior and amateur careers of Jones and Tiger Woods, their family and social backgrounds are worlds apart. Born March 17, 1902, Jones's father, Col. Robert Purmedus Jones, was a prominent Atlanta lawyer. As distinctly different as their backgrounds are, there are some interesting similarities between the relationships of the fathers and sons. Both fathers were accomplished baseball players and considered careers in professional baseball. Bobby Jones's grandfather, Robert Tyre Jones, threatened to disown Robert P. Jones if he signed a minor league baseball contract, just as Earl, Jones stayed on and graduated college instead.[3] Both fathers had close relationships with their sons, functioning both as friends and mentors. While Robert P. Jones was a colonel in nickname only, Earl actually attained the rank of lieutenant colonel.

The Jones family spent summers across the street from the Atlanta Country Club's East Lake Golf Course; the young Jones learned to play golf copying the swing of East Lake's professional Stewart Maiden, who had emigrated to America at the turn of the century.[4] By the age of six Jones won the East Lake Children's Tournament. He graduated from Georgia Institute of Technology with a mechanical engineering major, then Harvard with a graduate degree in English, and after only one year at Emory University Law School, passed the Georgia State Bar and joined his father's law firm.

Over a 17 year period between 1923 and 1930 Jones competed in 52 tournaments and won 23 of them, culminating in what was then referred to as the Grand Slam. In 1930, as an amateur, Jones won the U.S. Amateur, the British Amateur, the U.S. Open and the British Open Championships. At the time, these were the most prestigious golf championships, referred to as the Majors. Over the course of his career, he would win 12 major championships, second only to Jack Nicklaus, who won 20 majors during his career. It was this record of Nicklaus's that first inspired Tiger Woods as a child. The modern Grand Slam consists of the U.S. Open, the British Open, the American PGA Championship and the Masters.[5] Amateurs can compete in all of the Majors except for the PGA Championship, and they are all contested under a stroke (or medal[6]) play format.

There are two principal types of competition in the game of golf, match play and medal play. The former is played by comparing the score of each player after each hole—the lowest score wins the hole. The winner is the player who wins the most holes in an 18-hole match. When one player is ahead (or "up") by more holes than there are remaining to play, they are declared the winner, three holes up with two holes to play, or three and two. If a player is up as many holes as there are holes remaining, the player is said to be "dormie."[7] Throughout the early history of the game, match play was the most popular method of scoring both in competition and in social matches. Today, virtually all professional competitions are played as medal, or stroke play events.

There are some different rules applying to match play that do not apply to medal play competition. For example, the score in match play is only kept for the individual holes, not the entire 18 holes. So in match play a player may shoot a significantly lower score than his opponent for 18 holes, and still be defeated. A good analogy is the electoral college for the American presidential elections. It is possible, as was the case in the 2000 election, for a candidate to have a smaller popular vote across the country and still be elected president, as long as he wins the most populous states.

It was the advent of televised golf that changed the format of professional tournaments. While the head-to-head competition of match play truly tests the skill of one golfer against another, medal play assures that most of the players will be playing for the full four days of a professional tournament. This guarantees the commercial sponsors of tournaments a sufficient number of so-called marquee players on Sunday afternoon, and usually higher television ratings. It is regularly demonstrated, for example, that when Tiger Woods is competing in a tournament, the television ratings for that tournament will increase significantly. If these tournaments were match play, and Tiger was eliminated, the ratings would drop and the sponsor would have to be compensated. It was the monumental appeal and charisma of Arnold Palmer, who gained popularity just as televised golf was evolving in the late 1950s that sounded the death knell for match play in major championship golf. The U.S. Amateur remains one of the few televised championships to be contested using the match play format.

Anyone with a handicap of 2.4 or below is eligible to apply for the Amateur competition. Golf handicaps are determined by taking the 10 best scores of a player's most recent 20 scores and, based on a mathematical formula, assigning a handicap number. It allows players of widely different abilities to compete fairly against each other. There are regional qualifying sites for the Amateur throughout the country. A certain number of players from each of the regional qualifiers advance to the medal play competition of the Amateur. Those players play a two-day, 36-hole medal play competition and the lowest 64 players advance to the match play rounds. The players are seeded according to their medal play score, so the lowest score plays the highest score, the second lowest score plays the second highest score. To become the Amateur Champions, a player must qualify for the match play rounds, and then win six matches.

By virtue of winning the USGA Junior Championship Tiger qualified for the 1992 and 1993 USGA Amateur Championships. He managed to make the 64-player field through medal play both years, but was eliminated in the first and second round of match play respectively. While he didn't advance very far in either of these tournaments, he did gain experience that would be valuable in his subsequent attempts for the title.

Tiger had to qualify for the 1994 Amateur like any other golfer. The site he was assigned was in California, and circumstances had him and his father in Chicago the day before the qualifier. Earl and Tiger were late getting to the airport and missed the flight. They were put on a standby list for the next flight that was oversold. They were mistakenly given tickets which should have gone to a couple with the same last name, and when the Woods politely gave up the seats, even though it meant it would be virtually impossible for Tiger to have a chance to qualify for the Amateur, the airline personnel were so impressed with their attitude, they moved them to the top of the standby list. They eventually got on a plane and Tiger was able to make the qualifier—which he did as the medalist (low qualifier), after very little sleep.[8]

1994 AMATEUR

The 1994 Amateur was played at Tournament Players Club (TPC) at Sawgrass, in Jacksonville, Florida. This golf course is one of a number of courses designed and run by the professional golfing community. The Professional Golfers Association of America is the governing body of all professional golfers in the United States. Established in 1916, both touring professionals and club professionals belonged to the PGA. But by the late 1960s it was becoming increasingly apparent that the needs of the touring pros and the club pros were often at cross purposes. Consequently, in 1968 the Tournament Players Division split off from the PGA and became the Tournament Players Tour, as a sister organization that is made up exclusively of touring professionals. The TPC courses are owned and run by the Tournament Players Tour, and they are characterized as being fan-friendly (with plenty of vantage points from which spectators can view tournament golf) and as being the ultimate test for the highest caliber of golfer. The 17th hole at TPC Sawgrass is the signature hole that represents the challenge of all TPC courses. A short par three (up to 156 yards, depending on where the hole is placed), the hole requires players to shoot to a green completely surrounded by water. The relatively small target, coupled with the ever-changing Florida winds, make this hole one of the most entertaining on the PGA Tour. This was the venue that Tiger would face as he attempted to win his first U.S. Amateur.

Tiger's first opponent in the matches was Vaughn Moise, a 46 year old rules official, whom he defeated easily two and one. He then met Michael Flynn and had little trouble defeating him six and five. Tiger's next opponent in the round of 16 provided the closest match so far in the tournament. His opponent Buddy Alexander, was an older player and coach of the University of Florida golf team. Alexander was three up after 12 holes, and considering his experience and the psychological advantage he had over Tiger, there was every reason to believe that Tiger could lose. However, the mental training that Earl had drilled into Tiger as a boy allowed Tiger to overcome all disadvantages. Alexander had a short three-foot putt to go "dormie" on the 14th, but the putt lipped out of the hole. By this time a large crowd of clearly partisan Gator fans were following the match, and the press scrutiny of this young African American's career was increasing every time he played. Even though consideration of his race had been largely accepted by the public, this was still about an hour and a half from the university campus in Gainesville, Florida. A man in the crowd was overheard saying, "Who do you think these people are rooting for, the nigger or the Gator coach?"[9]

They arrived at the famous 17 hole all square. Rather than playing for the safe portion of the green, as most players, including Alexander, had done, Tiger hit his nine iron into the breeze right at the hole. The ball hovered over the water before settling on the fringe of the green, within three feet of the bulkhead guarding the water hazard. Alexander three putted from twenty-eight feet, and Tiger chipped to within two feet and sank the putt to win the hole. Both players double-bogeyed the final hole and Tiger won the match one up.

The quarter-final and semifinal matches were relatively easy for Tiger. In the quarter-final his opponent was Tim Jackson from Tennessee, and in the semifinal, Tim Frishette of Ohio. Tiger defeated them both five and four. Between these two matches, Tiger, uncertain about the consistency of his driving, contacted his coach, Butch Harmon, who was able to give him advice over the phone to solve the problem.

In his first U.S. Amateur final match, Tiger faced Trip Kuehne. Tiger and Earl were friends of the Kuehne family, and Tiger and Trip's younger sister Kelli (who was to become a standout college golfer, and later LPGA touring professional) were good friends. Trip's younger brother Hank Kuehne also became a professional golfer, one of the longest drivers currently on the PGA Tour. Tiger was down by six holes after the morning 18-hole round, and five up with 12 holes remaining. On the 17th hole (the 35th of the match) Tiger hit a soft wedge shot to the 138 yard par three hole. It stopped eight inches from a bulkhead guarding the water. He holed a 14-foot putt and was one up going to the final hole. Tiger won the 18th and became the youngest winner in the history of the Amateur.

His victory generated significant national attention. Tiger received letters from then-President Bill Clinton, Gary Player, Jesse Jackson and entertainer Sinbad. Jay Leno and David Letterman wanted him to appear on their programs; he declined. He also received a congratulatory letter from Phil Knight, president of Nike—who obviously didn't mind the fact that Tiger wore Reebok golf shoes during the Amateur final.

1995 AMATEUR

Nineteen ninety-five marked the 100th anniversary of the United States Golf Association, and in tribute the U.S. Amateur was staged at the Newport Golf Club in Rhode Island, one of the charter members of the organization, and the site of the first Amateur. Only eight players had won the Amateur two years in a row, and Jack Nicklaus was not one of them. This fact was extra motivation for the defending Amateur champion. For Tiger, this tournament represented another goal: the opportunity to win five consecutive USGA championships in a row—only Bobby Jones had won more.

After a good opening round of 68, that could have been lower if he putted better, Tiger nearly didn't make the 64 player field to continue in the match play competition when he shot 75 for the second round. In the next five matches Tiger had trouble only in the semifinal when he played Mark Plummer. The competition in the Amateur is a mixture of well-coached college players, former college players, occasional former professionals who have regained their amateur status, and some golfers who were pretty much self-taught and schooled on less-than-glamorous golf courses. Plummer, a 43 year old with a swing that NBC commentator Johnny Miller said, "...only a mother could love,"[10] had failed in gaining a PGA card and regained his amateur status. But despite his uncanny ability to get up and down from any place on the golf course, and eight one-putt greens, Tiger won this semifinal match two up on the 18th hole.

George "Buddy" Martucci was Tiger's opponent in the final match. Martucci was a 43-year-old Mercedes-Benz dealer and member of Pine Valley, Merion, and Seminole, three of the most exclusive American country clubs. He was an experienced match play player, and not likely to be intimidated by Tiger's reputation. Tiger was two down when they broke for lunch after the morning 18. By the 26th hole Tiger was leading, but Martucci evened the match at the 29th hole. Woods was one up going into the 36th and final hole. Martucci hit his approach shot about 20 feet from the hole. With the pressure squarely on the young Tiger, he hit a shot that significantly contributed to his growing legend. The previous spring, Tiger had been criticized by the press for his modest performance at the Masters. While he impressed everyone with his prodigious drives, the general consensus was that he was unable to control the distance of his approach shots—that he lacked finesse. Partially in response to the criticism, but mostly because of his obsessive desire to improve his game, he had practiced many hours to develop more control over how far he hit his iron shots. This 140 yard shot, to an elevated green, was exactly the kind of shot he had been practicing. Now it was time to hit under excruciating pressure. He did. The ball came off his eight iron club and floated on the breeze traveling exactly 18 inches farther than he calculated, and directly at the hole. Martucci conceded the putt, and the match was over.[11]

1996 AMATEUR

In the history of the Amateur nobody had ever won the championship three consecutive times. Bobby Jones won the tournament five times during his career, but never three times in a row. So the stakes were already established as Tiger prepared once again to make history at the Ghost Creek Course at Pumpkin Ridge, Oregon, site of the 1996 U.S. Amateur.

This would be the first Amateur that Tiger's mother would see him win. Because of the anticipated crowds, tournament officials allowed Kultida to go inside the ropes, which made it possible for her to watch her son compete. Throughout his amateur career, Tiger and his parents had maintained fairly good relations with the USGA. As early as the 1896 Open when USGA president, Theodore Havemeyer, insisted that an African American player should be allowed to compete, the organization had championed the rights of minorities in golf. During Tiger's junior career, the USGA had also loosened some restrictions on travel expenses, allowing for a child and a parent to travel to junior competitions and still retain amateur status. However, some critics of the Woods family complained that these changes were done specifically to allow Tiger to compete in more tournaments. The USGA denied this.

Earlier, Earl had been peeved when he had to pay $300 extra to change the dates for airline tickets he had purchased because the scheduled starting date for the Amateur was changed, and neither he nor Tiger had taken notice. As it turned out, this would be the last time Earl or Tiger would worry about the price of airline tickets, or any other expenses, for that matter.[12] This would be Tiger's last amateur competition.

There were 311 golfers trying to qualify for the 64 match play slots. Tiger shot 69, 67, and was the medalist. As if there wasn't already a considerable amount of pressure, only once in the previous 55 years had the medalist gone on to win the Amateur championship, and in the previous 10 years, only Phil Mickelsen, in 1990, had accomplished it.

It has been well documented that Tiger Woods had a diet similar to most young men of his age, and fruits and vegetables did not make up a substantial percentage of his calories. In Oregon, he would make a nightly stop at the local McDonalds on the way back to his hotel. Aware of his celebrity presence, the staff put up a picture of Tiger and began to list his daily intake of Big Macs and Egg McMuffins for the entire McDonald's clientele to peruse.[13]

Tiger faced J.D. Manning in his first match. Manning was a senior at Colorado State University. Tiger was in control of the match throughout, but undoubtedly the highlight was a shot he fashioned on the eight hole. Tiger's ball was on the fringe of the green right up against the collar of the green, making it virtually impossible to get the face of the putter on the ball. Indicative of his ability to create shots as the need arose, he took a pitching wedge, a very lofted club, and struck the ball with the sole of the club in the center of the ball and holed out the shot. Tiger went on to win three and two.

Tiger's next match was with Jerry Courville, the reigning Mid-Am Champion,[14] from Milford, Connecticut. A 37-year-old coordinator for Pitney Bowes, Courville had accumulated an impressive number of amateur golf titles both in Metropolitan Golf Association (MGA) and USGA competitions. As with many of his previous opponents, Courville's vast tournament experience should have put Tiger at a distinct disadvantage, however Woods birdied six of the final nine holes to defeat Courville four and three.

The next match featured Tiger against 14-year-old Charles Howell, the first opponent who was younger than Woods. In his short career Howell had demonstrated considerable promise, prompting Earl Woods to comment that he, if anybody, could match Tiger's Junior Amateur record. His age and sense of humor were reflected in response to a question on his Amateur application. Howell wrote that he had a superstition about walking under moving cars.[15] At the conclusion of the match, which Tiger won three and one, Howell said that he didn't lose ten and eight (the maximum margin of defeat possible in an 18-hole match), so he considered it a good day. Charles Howell would never win the Amateur, but he has gone on to play professional golf and to date has won three tournaments on the PGA Tour.

In the quarter final match, D.A. Points, a sophomore at Louisiana State University, was Tiger's competition. On the 12th hole, a par three with the hole cut dangerously close to a pond adjacent to the green, Points played the prescribed shot that dictated he hit his ball to the fat portion of the green, away from the trouble. Tiger aimed and hit his shot at the hole and it wound up leaving him a six-foot putt, which he made to go three up in the match. He eventually won three and two. This win set up a semifinal match between Tiger and his Stanford teammate and friend Joel Kribel.

Kribel was certainly not awed by Tiger. Kribel had been playing well during the summer, and had won two of the most prestigious amateur tournaments, the Western Amateur and the Pacific Northwest Amateur. He and Tiger competed on the same college team and had roomed together when the Cardinal team traveled to matches. Despite their close off-course relationship, Tiger virtually ignored his opponent, an indication of his unique ability to concentrate on the matter at hand. In reviewing comments by his teammates at Stanford, there is clearly a sense that they were uncomfortable with this side of Tiger's personality, but they all agree that it's the reason he was able to win so consistently.

At first Kribel showed no signs that Tiger's concentration was bothering him. He birdied the first hole and went two up through ten holes. However, he was unable to persevere. The combination of outstanding play by Tiger—he didn't bogie a hole, in fact he went 116 holes without a bogey during the tournament—and less than stellar play from Kribel, meant that Tiger was able to take control of the match. The only birdie by Kribel scored, on the 14th hole, was countered by an eagle from Tiger. Woods defeated his teammate three and one, to set up the historic final for the Amateur Championship.

Up to this time, the final of the U.S. Amateur generally was not considered a marquee event on television. In 1981, the late Bing Crosby's son Nathaniel won the Amateur final defeating Brian Undley, and this attracted some national television attention. Normally, the event was carried for the hardcore golf fans, and was usually part of a package that help ensure a network's bid to the USGA to obtain the rights to carry the more ratings-friendly U.S. Open Tournament. Tiger's opponent, Steve Scott, was a 19-year-old college sophomore from the University of Florida who suddenly found himself in the middle of a national spectacle. And to add contrast to the match, Scott's girlfriend, Kristi Hommel caddied for him. So on one side there was Team Tiger with Butch Harmon working with Tiger on the practice tee, and on the other Scott's girlfriend massaging his neck between shots. There were a considerable number of people pulling for the couple—against great odds.

But Scott's David was up to the challenges of Tiger's Goliath. The challenger was five holes up after the morning eighteen. Scott continued to put on the pressure with some miraculous shots to win and halve holes. It came down to the 17th hole with Tiger one down. He was feet from the hole and, despite the immense pressure, rolled the putt in to tie the match. On the 18th hole, both players made pars, so the match went into a playoff. After matching pars on the 37th hole, Scott stumbled and missed a six-foot putt to bogey and Tiger stroked in a short par putt to win.

Beyond the interest in Tiger's record setting-performance, the story getting more attention was whether this would be Tiger's last amateur competition. At this time there were rumors that he was planning to leave college and turn professional after the Amateur. But before considering the implications of that transition, it is necessary to examine the circumstances surrounding the college recruiting process and impact of Tiger's two years at Stanford University.

COLLEGE GOLF

Tiger Woods had good grades in high school; he could go to college pretty much anywhere he wanted. In addition to his solid academic record and golfing prowess he was a member of the Honor Society. He was recruited by a number of colleges, but it ultimately came down to University of Nevada-Las Vegas and Stanford. Stanford's golf coach Wally Goodwin had contacted Tiger before he was in high school to tell him about the golf program at Stanford. In addition to a reputation for excellence in Division I athletics, Stanford ranks in the top echelon of America's competitive academic universities. It annually ranks among the top institutions for graduation rates of athletes.[16] These factors were all important, not only to Tiger and Earl, but also Kultida, who was adamant that Tiger get a college degree, and she influenced his decision in his senior year at Western High School to select Stanford.

Having won the U.S. Amateur before college, Tiger was already a celebrity before entering Stanford, but the university was not at a loss for highly talented students. In his class were actor Fred Savage, who starred in the long-running television series *The Wonder Years*, and Olympic gymnast Dominique Dawes.[17] His team was not without some talented golfers as well. Two of his teammates, Casey Martin and Notah Begay, have gone on to significant careers, and both have garnered their own degree of celebrity.

Martin was an upperclassman when Tiger came to Stanford. Winner of 17 junior titles in Oregon, Martin suffered from Klippel-Trenaunay-Weber Syndrome, a rare circulatory disease that made it difficult for him to walk. After graduating from Stanford, Martin pursued a career in professional golf. However, due to tournament rules against riding in a golf cart during competition, he couldn't compete in PGA or USGA tournaments. Martin challenged the rules and the case went ultimately to the United States Supreme Court. The high court ruled seven to two in his favor in 2001.[18] Martin had been granted an injunction and was allowed to use a cart on the PGA Tour, and has otherwise been successful on the Nationwide Tour, made up of a series of smaller tournaments for players who have not earned PGA Tour playing privileges.

Notah Begay, the most successful Native American golfer, with four PGA Tour victories, is half Navajo, one-quarter San Felipe, and one-quarter Isleta. After a successful start on the PGA Tour, in January 2000 Begay was arrested and pled guilty to driving- while-intoxicated charges. He subsequently talked openly about his problems with alcohol and how he dealt with them. He is currently on medical exemption from the Tour because of chronic back problems.[19]

Despite an unprecedented buildup to his arrival at Stanford, Tiger functioned as any freshman would. He was regularly relegated to the back of the line by the upperclassmen on the golf team. When they traveled on road trips he would inevitably be assigned the rollaway bed in the hotel. Tiger pledged for Sigma Chi fraternity, and participated in the normal schedule of parties. One of his fraternity brothers was quoted as saying, "...Tiger Woods is probably the greatest golfer of all time, but he is probably the worst dancer."[20] He more or less blended in with the student population and was able to gain a certain amount of anonymity at Stanford. Freshmen at the university are assigned roommates at random, and it happened that Tiger's roommate knew nothing about golf. He once told Tiger he had a phone call from somebody with a funny accent. It turned out to be Australian Greg Norman calling to arrange for a practice round at Augusta National.[21]

From the beginning, Tiger showed that he would not be intimidated by collegiate competition. He won the first college tournament he entered (it actually took place a week before the fall term started), the William Tucker Invitational. He placed fifth in the NCAA Championships, and was named Stanford Male Freshman of the Year. He was selected as a preseason First Team, All-American by *Golfweek* magazine, and then was named to their First Team, All-American (at the end of the season).[22] Probably the most satisfying victory in Tiger's collegiate career occurred at the Jerry Pate Invitational tournament, at the Shoal Creek in Alabama.

The club had been at the center of the controversy alluded to earlier when, on the eve of the 1990 PGA Championship at the club, Hall Thompson, the club's president, stated that there were no black members in Shoal Creek, and there wouldn't be. Tiger was only 15 at the time, and wasn't fully aware of the controversy. However, even as a college freshman, he understood completely the opportunity he had to score a symbolic victory for racial tolerance. Ironically, an African American group threatened to protest Tiger's participation, claiming that he should not play at this club that had only allowed an honorary black member in order to play the PGA tournament in 1990. Tiger did compete, and in a growing body of evidence that he was able to completely filter out outside distractions when he was on a golf course, he shot 67 and won the tournament by two strokes.[23]

Only Jack Nicklaus and Phil Mickelsen had ever won both the U.S. Amateur and the NCAA Championships—Mickelsen in the same year—so this goal was clearly in Tiger's sights. However, due to some illnesses and injuries earlier in the spring of 1995, Tiger had not practiced with the usual intensity and his game was not its sharpest. In the NCAA Championships he shot four respectable rounds but finished fifth. Assuming that he stayed in school for four years, he would have three more opportunities to join Nicklaus and Mickelsen as Amateur-NCAA winners.

His second year confirmed that he was the dominant amateur player in America. The big college tournaments were the Pac 10 Championships, the NCAA Regionals and the NCAA Championships. All three were to be played at courses where Tiger had played and was familiar with.[24] It was at the Pac 10 Championships where Tiger had one of his finest days on a golf course. In the morning 18-hole round he broke the course and Pac 10 record, and equaled the NCAA record when he shot 61. After a 15-minute rest in the 90 degree heat, he went out and shot 65. He won the individual title by 14 strokes, and Stanford placed eighth. But the culmination of his college career was to be the NCAA Championships held at the Honors Course at Ooltewah, Tennessee. Tiger trailed by one stroke after the first round shooting 69, when Pat Perez of Arizona State University broke the course record with a score of 68. By the end of the day, that record was shattered when Tiger shot 67, giving him a five-shot lead. A third round 69 gave him a nine-shot lead, and even though he faltered and shot 80 on the last day he won the individual title by four strokes.

In addition to being selected to every All-American college golf team, Tiger won the Jack Nicklaus Award for the top male collegiate Golfer of the Year, the Fred Haskins Award and the Pac 10 Golfer of the Year.

But his experiences at Stanford were not all positive. One night when returning from a campus party he was mugged by a man with a knife. The assailant took his watch and a gold chain and struck him with the handle of the knife. He was not hurt, but the fact that the perpetrator used Tiger's name during the assault was unsettling to both Tiger and Earl.[25] And he continued to get letters that could only be called hate mail. One anonymous letter he showed a teammate read, "You can take the nigger out of the jungle, but you can't take the jungle out of the nigger."[26] This kind of letter clearly seemed to indicate that despite the general acceptance of African American athletes in most other sports, there was something different about golf.

Tiger and Earl also continued to have problems with the governing body of intercollegiate athletics, the NCAA, and by default the Stanford athletic administration. As indicated earlier, two years before Tiger attended Stanford he had had a run-in with the NCAA when Tiger was offered an honorary membership in the Big Canyon Golf Club. The NCAA first said that he couldn't accept, and then relented. Another incident that further defined the relationship between the Woods family and the NCAA involved a controversy over Tiger's having dinner with Arnold Palmer. Tiger had the opportunity to meet Palmer when he won his first Junior Amateur Championship in 1991 at Palmer's Bay Hill course in Florida. They had communicated by mail and phone over the years, and when Palmer was scheduled to participate in a senior tournament in California, Tiger contacted him to see if they could meet to talk. Tiger sought advice about the ever-increasing speculation that Tiger would some day assume Palmer's unofficial role of ambassador of golf. Arrangements were made for Tiger to drive to Napa Valley to have dinner with Mr. Palmer. They met, had dinner and a most valuable exchange of information about Palmer's career and its parallels to Tiger's. When the bill came, Palmer picked up the check, despite Tiger's offer to pay for his portion of the bill.

Tiger was shocked when someone showed him a newspaper with a headline indicating that the dinner was apparently a potential violation of NCAA rules. Wally Goodwin, Tiger's coach, immediately suspended him pending a reply from the NCAA. Both Earl and Kultida were surprised and angered. They wondered why the coach did not attempt to find out more about the circumstances that led to the dinner and Palmer's largesse. The situation was exacerbated by the fact that Tiger's parents could not talk directly with the NCAA, whose rules required them to deal with a compliance officer at Stanford, who could tell them nothing. In frustration, Kultida finally contacted some members of the press to explain what had happened. It's difficult to determine exactly why, but eventually the NCAA determined that since Tiger had known Palmer as a friend before the dinner, he would not be suspended. Earl wondered why these facts could not have been gathered before Tiger was suspended from the team.[27]

Throughout his junior career, Tiger had regularly staged instructional clinics, coordinated by Earl, and generally in areas where there were few opportunities for kids to have access to golfing facilities or instruction. When Tiger came under the sanctions of the NCAA, he was prohibited from individually conducting clinics, farther than 30 miles from Stanford. Earl Woods sarcastically notes in his book that these rules were probably formulated when the farthest one could travel in a day was by horse and buggy.[28] The rules, however, did allow for individual institutions to sponsor clinics anywhere, so Tiger did a number of clinics with the Stanford golf team. During the 1995 Masters Tournament, Tiger had written a series of diary entries published in the *Golf Week* and *Golf World* magazines recounting his experiences as an amateur at the Masters. Even though he was not paid for the writing, he was suspended by Stanford for one day.

While Tiger was at Stanford Earl began writing his first book, *Training A Tiger,* and he tried to contact both the NCAA and the USGA to find out what Tiger could do in connection with the publication and promotion of the book. According to Earl, the USGA informed them that in order for Tiger to retain his amateur status, he could not appear on the cover of the book, but he could pose for instructional photographs and he could write a foreword, but he couldn't make appearances promoting the book. The NCAA, through Stanford's compliance officer—since technically Earl could not communicate directly with the NCAA—said pretty much the same as the USGA, but Earl's perception of their abuse of power drove Tiger closer and closer to his decision to turn professional.

Tiger's parents were not the first to question the almost dictatorial power of the NCAA that made member institutions afraid of even the threat of a sanction. Since his problems with the NCAA, the organization has instituted a series of reforms to try and address some of the issues of granting more local control to the member institutions. However, an inextricable bond has been forged between intercollegiate athletics and commerce, and mere adjustments in the system have not significantly alleviated the problem. Given the immense financial benefits reaped by academic institutions from intercollegiate athletics, there is little incentive to change the system. The time has come to deal honestly with student-athletes as part of the public relations/development arm of academic institutions. Just as accommodations are made for special students (i.e., older women returning to school, students with learning disabilities, handicapped students), athletes should be granted similar accommodations. They should have classes only when they are not in season, and they should be paid enough to eliminate the attraction of unauthorized cash and amenities.

But to be fair, Tiger Woods presented a unique situation for amateur athletics in general. Never before had there been such interest and commercial potential anticipated for an amateur athlete. So while Earl's frustrations are understandable, both organizations defining amateur status were operating in virtually uncharted waters. And the fact that Earl had been contracted by IMG early in Tiger's career to scout junior golf prospects didn't help the situation. Regardless of the right and wrong on both sides, for the purposes of the fate of Tiger Woods's amateur career, the damage had already been done.

THE PROFESSIONAL

It was apparent by the summer of 1996 that Tiger Woods was ready to play professional golf. Even though he had not yet contended in any of the professional tournaments he played as an amateur, he was physically mature and, at least as far as golf was concerned, emotionally ready to compete on a higher level. But both Tiger's parents were adamantly committed to his finishing college, since both their families recognized the value of education. Butch Harmon, his coach, was against Tiger turning pro at this time. Harmon told him he should have fun in college; the opportunity was once in a lifetime. And Tiger enjoyed his years at Stanford. He enjoyed the camaraderie of his teammates, and was fully engaged in both his academic studies and the social life of a college campus. He had spoken to many of his teammates throughout the year about the possibility of turning pro, but would never disclose his future plans. It's difficult to say whether he would have stayed in college and graduated had he not encountered so many problems with the NCAA, and to a lesser extent the USGA amateur guidelines.

Tiger's mother and father made him promise that if he left Stanford that he would finish college at some time in the future. Jack Nicklaus never went back and finished his degree at Ohio State University when he left to become a golf professional, and since Tiger was constantly comparing himself to Nicklaus, this fact undoubtedly influenced his ultimate decision. Nicklaus had declared Tiger to be the "next Nicklaus." However, some speculated that Nicklaus made the pronouncement to exert pressure that might prohibit his prophesy. After all, Tiger was not the first "next" Nicklaus. There had been many promising young golfers who never lived up to the hype—Tom Weiskopf and Andy Bean among them.

Tiger's performance at the 1996 British Open demonstrated that he was ready to make the transition. He shot 75 the first day of the Open and afterwards, Jack Nicklaus gave him a stern talking-to that impressed Tiger. Nicklaus told him that he had to put the same intense concentration on the first day of a tournament as the last. Tournaments are not won on the first day, but they are lost.[29]

In retrospect, Tiger's decision to become a professional seems like a foregone conclusion. However, in 17 professional tournaments he competed in as an amateur he only made seven cuts. So there was still a question as to whether he would make the transition successfully. There was no such doubt among potential agents and corporate sponsors. Early in Tiger's junior career, IMG had exhibited interest in Tiger as a client. During that time Earl Woods was hired by IMG to serve as a scout for potential talent in the junior golf ranks. A cynical view might see this arrangement as an early guarantee that Tiger would sign with the company as his representative. Hughes Norton was one of the principals at IMG and early on he had befriended Earl.[30]

Immediately following his victory at the 1996 Amateur, rumors began to circulate that Tiger would turn professional. While Tiger wanted to make a formal announcement at a press conference at the Brown Deer Park Golf course, site of the Milwaukee Open, where he was scheduled to play as an amateur in the Wednesday Pro-Am, a secret like this inevitably would be leaked, and it was. So on the Tuesday before the start of the tournament Tiger was forced to issue a press release with the following statement: "This is to confirm that, as of now, I am a professional golfer. I will not answer any questions, or have any further comment until tomorrow at 2:30 P.M. at my scheduled press conference. I would appreciate the media respecting my wishes to practice without distractions today. I will be available to answer your questions tomorrow."[31]

There were, of course, many corporations that were interested in snagging Tiger Woods to endorse their products. Speculations about the size of potential deals were in the $5-million-a-year-for-five-years category. The final major deal was with Nike for $40 million for five years, including a $7.5 million signing bonus. Phil Knight, the CEO of Nike, was questioned about the prospects of spending that much money on a golfer who had never teed up a ball as a professional, but he said that the preprofessional promotion had been so overwhelming that it was not such a gamble.

A deal was also cut with Titleist, manufacturer of golf balls and other golf equipment. Tiger was paid $3 million to play the Titleist golf ball and other Titleist equipment (i.e., gloves, golf bag). Eventually Titleist began manufacturing golf clubs and paid Tiger additional money to use their clubs, but for the time being he was able to stay with the Mizuno irons, the clubs he had used throughout most of his amateur career.

Once again Tiger had bested Jack Nicklaus. In 1961 when Nicklaus left Ohio State to become a professional golfer he received $450,000 for five years from the MacGregor (golf equipment) Company. The deal included a $100,000 signing bonus, $100,000 in guaranteed royalties, and $50,000 a year for five years. Adjusted for 1996 monetary standards, Nicklaus' package was about $500,000 a year. Tiger's deal produced just under $9 million a year. In addition to signifying Tiger's tremendous appeal, these figures are also indicative of the tremendous increase in interest in sports (brought on largely by television) and the sport of golf in 47 years.[32] ABC golf producer Jack Graham pointed to the 5.3 overnight rating garnered at Tiger's dramatic win at the Amateur, against a rival network's golf telecast featuring PGA stars Greg Norman and Phil Mickelesen.[33] These deals made Tiger among the highest-paid professional athletes. Michael Jordan remained the highest-paid athlete, at about $40 million for 1996, while Tiger (before the Titleist deal) was ranked 25th. An indication of the rapid transition from an amateur to wealthy professional is demonstrated in an incident described by Butch Harmon, who had to lend Tiger the money to pay the entry fee to the Milwaukee Open because he hadn't yet opened a checking account.[34] Another time Harmon and Tiger went out to buy some clothes at a mall. When the salesperson rang up the total Tiger handed her a credit card. It didn't go through, so he handed her another credit card, and it didn't go through. Harmon asked him if he had activated the cards, and Tiger asked, "What's that?"[35]

The much anticipated press conference in Milwaukee had to be moved to a larger venue as the requests for media credentials had doubled from the previous year. There were representatives from *Time*, *People* magazine and television's *Extra*. Tiger read from a statement:

> ...Several weeks ago I spoke with some very special people, my parents, and told them after a frustrating and painful process, I was struggling with the decision to become a professional golfer. Then I spoke with a few very close friends, whose advice and counsel I trust and respect, and told them of my thoughts. The reaction of both my parents and friends were similar...they asked serious questions, offered their views, then, after heated debate, especially by my dad, told me they would fully support any decision I made.[36]

After Tiger's press conference Earl stayed and talked to the press, who were understandably anxious to get some quotes. Unfortunately, Earl was obliging. He stated that there was no comparison between Tiger and Muhammad Ali, or Arthur Ashe since Tiger would have an impact beyond sports. He boasted that if Tiger wasn't playing golf he would be a premier 400 meter runner, who would beat the current Olympic champion (Michael Johnson, whom Earl referred to as Michael Jackson), and finally, in describing Tiger's killer instinct, he drew an analogy between Tiger and a Western black gunslinger.[37] Putting aside a father's obvious pride in his son's accomplishments, Earl's quotes made it no easier for Tiger, who was already facing some resistance from his fellow professionals.

The reception for Tiger Woods as a newcomer by his fellow professionals was, at best, mixed. Generally the established stars accepted him and recognized that his presence would reinvigorate the public's interest in the game, and eventually lead to higher television ratings and more prize money. However, there were less-recognizable names who resented the fact that all this money was going to player who had yet to pay any dues to the tour.

Not all the press was buying the supposed impromptu coming out of Tiger Woods on August 27, 1996. Writer John Feinstein questioned the spontaneity of Woods's opening line at the press conference in Milwaukee—"Well, I guess it's, hello world." Less than 48 hours later the line was part of a sophisticated ad campaign featuring Tiger, already filmed, using the line as a theme.[38] The subsequent ad campaign featured a three-page ad in *The Wall Street Journal* that pictured Tiger and the copy:

> I shot in the 70s when I was 8. I shot in the 60s when I was 12. I won the U.S. Junior Amateur when I was 14. I played in the Nissan Los Angeles Open when I was 16. I won the U.S. Amateur when I was 19. I am the only man to win three consecutive U.S. Amateur titles. There are still golf courses in the United States that I cannot play because of the color of my skin. I'm told I'm not ready for you. Are you ready for me?[39]

Woods shot a 67 in the first round at Milwaukee and 69 the second round. That put him eight shots behind the leaders. This was the beginning of Tiger's initiation into the world of the professional ranks. By the third round, the events of the previous week finally caught up with him. He was clearly exhausted and shot a 73 and was out of contention. During the third round, he gave a preview of the impact he would have on the PGA Tour when he made a hole-in-one from 202 yards. He would go on to shoot 68 and finish tied for 60th, earning $2,544. Tiger was pleased with his first attempt at professional golf. Despite the fact that he had just signed a $40 million endorsement deal, Tiger treasured this first check as the only money he had earned completely on his own.

There are several ways for a golfer to qualify to compete full time on the PGA Tour. While it was a virtual certainty that eventually Tiger Woods would qualify for the PGA Tour, the question was how he would do it and how quickly. As has been stated, the PGA Tour is a relatively recent phenomenon. It wasn't until Walter Hagen quit his job as head professional at Oakland Hills Golf Club following his victory in the 1919 U.S. Open that anyone could conceive of making a living playing tournament golf.[40] In fact Hagen made the most money playing exhibition matches throughout the world. The tour in Hagen's day consisted of a schedule of local and regional tournaments for small prize money. There was very little corporate sponsorship, and there wasn't television to generate mass interest in the sport. Most professional golfers of the period maintained some connection to a golf club for their main livelihood. For the really accomplished players, their responsibilities to the home club were minimal, because if they won, it brought publicity to their home course. The less-talented players had to serve as club professionals, giving lessons to the members, running club tournaments, and selling golf equipment. So in the early days on the Tour anybody who could come up with the entrance fee could play in the tournament. That has changed dramatically. It wasn't until the confluence of televised golf and the arrival of Arnold Palmer in the late 1950s that most of the players on the PGA Tour could earn a living playing in professional golf tournaments exclusively.

Given the number of golfers trying to become qualified to play on the PGA Tour, a special tournament qualifier is held every year to determine who will have the rights to play on the tour. To begin with, a player must have won at least two legitimate tournaments at the local level, either through their local or regional golf association, or the PGA Section in their part of the country. That allows them to register, after paying a $2,500 registration fee, to compete in a regional qualifier from which a designated number of the players with the lowest scores advance to the Qualifying School Finals. "Q" School Finals consist of six rounds and 108 holes. First the players must survive a 72-hole cut, from which the low 90 players advance to the final 72 holes. Only the top 26 finishers and ties are fully qualified to play on the PGA Tour the following year. The players scoring from 27th place to 77th place are qualified to play on the Nationwide Tour, which is a smaller tour with less money, prestige and television coverage. Qualifying through "Q" School only exempts a player for one year. Only the top 125 players on the PGA Money List earn an exemption for the following year. If a player doesn't make the Top 125 on the PGA Money List, they must go back to the Qualifying School. It is probably the most demanding selection process of any professional sport, and even if a player gains his tour card he is not guaranteed a salary.

The other way a player may participate in a PGA Tournament is by sponsors' exemptions. If a player gets enough sponsor's exemptions and is able to earn enough prize money to get into the top 125 list, he is declared eligible to compete on the tour for the year. This was the way Tiger would first try to qualify for the 1997 PGA Tour. However, he had a limited number of opportunities since there were relatively few tournaments left on the schedule. It wasn't a problem of getting sponsor's exemptions, since every tournament director was more than anxious to get Tiger to play in their tournament.

After his tie for 60th finish at the Milwaukee Tournament, Tiger was 334th on the PGA Money List. He would need to win about $250,000 more to gain exemption for the 1997 season.

The next event on the PGA Tour was the Canadian Open, played at the historic Glen Abbey Golf Club. Although this is the national championship of Canada, the prize money from this tournament counts toward the PGA Money List. The tournament was shortened to 54 holes because of inclement weather, but with the help of a tournament low round of 68 on the last day, Tiger was able to finish in 11th place and collect $37,500. He was now 204 on the money list.

The Quad City Open is held annually at the Oakwood Country Club. Four cities sponsor the event (Davenport and Bettendorf, Iowa, and Rock Island and Moline, Illinois) and that was the next stop on the PGA Tour. The tournament director was beside himself that Tiger was going to compete, and despite all the preparations they wound up using magic markers on people's hands because he ran out of tickets. Before the tournament, in an interview with Forrest Sawyer on ABC's *Nightline*, John Feinstein (as he had written in a *Newsweek* article) compared Earl Woods to then-fallen tennis prodigy Jennifer Capriati's father, Stephano. He noted that Earl hadn't had a job since 1988, and that he was living off his son.[41] This criticism overlooked the fact that Earl Woods had retired after what could only be called a distinguished military career, and that despite Earl's propensity for hyperbole, he was certainly capable of providing for himself and his family. Despite the distraction of this negative image, the Quad City Open proved to be a significant lesson for the emerging superstar.

Tiger was leading after the third round by one stroke over Ed Fiori, a journeyman pro, who was about to achieve the greatest moment in his professional career. Tiger hooked a ball off the fourth hole, a 460-yard par four into a pond. Rather than dropping a ball, taking the penalty and punching out onto the fairway to try and salvage a bogey, Tiger tried to make a virtually impossible shot through a narrow opening in the trees. The ball hit a tree and wound up in a swamp. Later in the round he was on the par four hole in two strokes, eight feet from the hole, and unbelievably, he four putted for double bogey. But he didn't give up. He finished tied for fifth and won $42,150 vaulting him up to 166th on the money list. Despite all his amateur triumphs, it was obvious that Tiger had to adjust to the rigors of PGA competition where the depth of talent in the players was deep. Also the field at the Quad City tournament was not particularly strong because it was scheduled against the President's Cup Tournament, where most of the top PGA players competed. The young golfer learned that over 72 holes, you sometimes have to cut your losses.

Most people unfamiliar with golf, if they care at all, would assume that the B.C. Open, next on Tiger's quest to gain his tour card, is played in British Columbia. Instead the now-defunct tournament was played in Endicott, New York and was named in honor of the B.C. cartoon, whose creator, Johnny Hart, lives in the town and is an avid supporter of the game, both in his cartoon and in real life. It too was hampered by bad weather, and resulted in a 54-hole winner, Fred Funk, who finished three strokes ahead of Tiger who was third. When asked what Tiger needed to be successful on the PGA Tour, Funk responded, "A good accountant."[42] The third place finish added $58,000 to his earnings and put him at 128th on the money list, and virtually assured that Tiger would be able to compete on the tour in 1997.

He withdrew from the next week's tournament, the Buick Open, which caused a considerable furor. This incident demonstrated that more would be expected of Tiger Woods than to play golf, and will be dealt with in Chapter 6.

The next tournament was the Las Vegas Invitational, played at three different golf courses. This tournament was unique in that it was contested over 90 holes rather than the normal 72. Tiger started steadily shooting 70 in the opening round and a brilliant 63 in the second round. His good play continued on Friday and Saturday when he shot 68 and 67 respectively. The extra day allowed Tiger to stay in contention despite the mediocre opening round. In the final round Tiger came to the final hole needing a par to tie Davis Love III, who was still on the course. He made par, and then had to wait and see if Love would be able to birdie to win. From the practice range, where Tiger refused to do any interviews, he struggled to maintain his concentration in case there was a playoff. Over one of the official's walkie-talkies, Tiger and his caddie "Fluff" Cowan heard that Love had an eight-foot birdie putt to win, and they listened as the voice on the other end informed them that the putt was missed. A playoff ensued.

Because of television contracts, the tradition of 18-hole playoffs had long ago become history. Television requires a drama, and the prospects of clearing lucrative afternoon network time on a Monday is not an option. Consequently most tour events stage a sudden-death playoff immediately following completion of play. Because the cameras traditionally cover the last few holes best, playoffs usually take place on those holes. This playoff at Las Vegas was contested on the 18th hole, and if they were still tied they would go to the 17th hole and then back to the 18th hole. The only tournament that retains an 18-hole playoff on the following day is the U.S. Open. The tradition-minded USGA has not yet given into the pressure of television.

Davis Love won the honors with a toss of a coin and used his driver, hitting the ball in the middle of the fairway. Tiger reached for a three wood, a more lofted club that would undoubtedly leave his drive farther from the hole than Love's. In golf, the player farthest from the hole plays first, and it was suggested later that Tiger used this tactic so that he would play first and try to get his ball on the green to put more pressure on his opponent, who was a much more experienced tournament golfer. Once again Tiger demonstrated that he had the instincts of a much more mature player. After hitting an eight iron about 18 feet from the hole, it was Love's turn to play. He swung too hard and his ball landed in a bunker over the green. After playing the bunker shot to within six feet of the hole, Tiger lagged his putt to within inches of the hole, thereby insuring a par for the hole. Love needed the six foot putt to tie the hole and prolong the playoff to the next hole. He missed and Tiger Woods, after only seven weeks on tour, at 20 years old, was the winner of his first championship on the PGA Tour. Tiger embraced his mother, who was at greenside.

Unfortunately for Earl, who was not in Las Vegas for the momentous occasion, ESPN, which was covering the tournament, opted to go back to the studios to start their pregame NFL football coverage, promising to show the playoff in its entirety during the football game. It was just not the same as seeing it live. It was probably the last time Tiger was preempted.[43] Tiger finished third at the following week's Texas Open, and if he won again he would be eligible for the Tour Championship, a $3 million event with a $540,000 first prize.

It was on to Florida and the Disney/Oldsmobile Classic. This was now Tiger's home—he had recently moved into the exclusive Ilesworth Community in Orlando. The tournament director of the Disney Classic, Michael McPhillips, had been courting Tiger to play in their tournament since he turned pro. He had been in constant touch with Hughes Norton, at one point phoning from his car that he was driving around Orlando with six strawberry milkshakes from McDonald's trying to find a drop point near Tiger's home.[44] Initially Tiger had said he wasn't going to play at Disney, but McPhillips continued to press, setting up newspaper copy announcing the arrival of Tiger, and even promising to allow Tiger to use a normally locked back gate of the golf course that would cut off 15 minutes from Tiger's daily commute to the tournament. When it was finally known that Tiger was going to play in the tournament, a whole new operational plan had to be put into effect. More programs had to be printed, additional security had to be enlisted, additional bleachers had to be constructed behind the practice area, and more buses added. The usual suspects from the press were joined by an influx of national media writers—*Sports Illustrated, Golf Magazine*, the *New York Times*, and probably the biggest winner of all, the Golf Channel, which had the rights to televise this tournament. The producers could only have speculated that Tiger Woods would turn professional before this event, and they certainly didn't know whether or not he would play in the tournament. The reason the Golf Channel secured the rights to this event in the first place was because it was normally a year-end attempt by the lesser known professionals to try and make the Top 125 Money List, and not of interest to the broadcast networks. The Golf Channel became the beneficiaries of the ratings bonanza.

In what was becoming his trademark slow start, Tiger shot 69 in the opening round. While he was well down the leader board, he was playing well and felt confident. The Disney tournament was played on several of the park's courses, so on Friday Tiger played the Lake Buena Vista course, and shot 63, which put him two shots from the leader. Tiger shot 69 on Saturday, and three-putted on the 18th hole to lose a share of the lead by one stroke. The final round of the tournament resulted in another Tiger win but not without some unusual incidents before it was over.

Tiger was paired with former U.S. Open Champion Payne Stewart, and the crowds following them were tremendous. As the twosome was going from the sixth to the seventh holes, the crowd, en masse, cut across a wooded area between the holes and startled a young deer who ran toward the swamp, whereupon a local alligator was apparently roused with the prospects of an early dinner. The deer didn't know which direction posed the most danger, and skittered off into the fields to escape the whole situation.

Unaware of the deer's plight, Tiger was busy on the golf course finishing his round in 66 strokes; Stewart shot 67 and it appeared Tiger had won his second tournament in eight weeks. But out on the course Taylor Smith, a relatively unknown young professional, still had a chance to tie Tiger. Earlier in the round, Smith's playing partner, Lennie Clement, had noticed that Smith was playing with a putter that had an illegal grip, and he reported the infraction to the PGA officials. Smith asked if he could continue playing while the Committee considered the situation, and they allowed him to do so. Smith eventually birdied the final hole to apparently tie Woods, but the Committee ruled that he be disqualified. Tiger expressed disappointment that Smith and he were not able to compete in a playoff.[45] This win boosted Tiger's winnings to $734,790 and gained him a spot in the Tour Championship the following week in Tulsa, Oklahoma. This tournament was restricted to the top 20 money winners on tour.

It was inevitable that comparisons with Jack Nicklaus would continue to be made. Tiger had finished in the top 10 in five of his first seven professional tournaments, winning two; Nicklaus had finished in the top 10 only once and had not won a single tournament in his debut on the tour. Woods had managed to achieve the most promising start of any golf professional in the history of the sport.

During this euphoric period Tiger's closest friend on tour, Mark O'Meara, had indicated that the time to judge the true greatness of Tiger Woods would be when he was not playing at his best and winning tournaments, but when adversity struck. That prediction was made reality during the Tour Championship in Tulsa, Okalahoma on October 25, 1996. After a serviceable opening round of 70 he was two strokes off the lead, anticipating his Friday 2:51 P.M. tee time for the second round. That night Earl Woods was admitted to the St. Francis Trauma Center, across the street from the hotel where Tiger and his family were staying, complaining of chest pains. Tiger didn't get to sleep until 5:00 A.M. and the following day went through the motions on the course, opening with par, double-bogey, and then proceeded to bogey five of the last six holes. But he didn't quit. Somehow he managed to shoot 35 on the back nine for a 78. His playing partner, the veteran John Cook, said,

> He showed me a lot today and it wasn't golf. You can lose your mind out here, and he didn't. To hold his demeanor like he did was more impressive to me than some of the drives he tried to hit. In a situation like that you could stomp off and complain, moan and act like a 20 year old but he didn't do that. He tried to make the best of a difficult day.[46]

It was not determined whether Earl was suffering from a mild heart attack or from a bronchial problem. He had had bypass surgery 10 years earlier, and had not made any serious attempts to curtail his unhealthy heart behavior—he still smoked and was overweight. Tiger managed to shoot 72 and 68 for the final two rounds and finished tied for 21st.

Tiger completed his abbreviated season 24 on the money list with a total of $790,594 in prize money. His average winnings-per-tournament was the highest on the tour, surpassing Tom Lehman, who at the time held the season-earnings record of $1.78 million. In 10 weeks Tiger had two victories.

Tiger continued his great play to begin the 1997 season. At the Mercedes he shot a 65 on Saturday, birdying the last four holes to tie 1996 Player of the Year, Tom Lehman. The following day a torrential downpour caused the officials to cancel the final round and stage a sudden-death playoff between Woods and Lehman. The playoff would be at the seventh hole, a par three with an elevated green, and about the only hole playable on the course. It required a shot completely over water. Lehman had the honor and, obviously not fully warmed up, hit his six iron shot into the water. The stunned crowd expected Tiger to play a conservative shot, since he could probably make a four and still win the tournament. In what was fast becoming a characteristic of his style of play he proceeded to hit a shot that came within six inches of going into the hole. After a penalty stroke Lehman dropped his ball and hit a shot that almost went in the hole, but even if it had, it was still only three. Tiger tapped in his birdie to win his third tournament. In spite of his amazing start on the PGA Tour, all eyes were on Tiger as he prepared to play in his first major championship as a professional. Winning regular tour championships assures a good living; winning major championships assures a place in golf history.

THE MASTERS RECORD

Although the Masters Tournament is the youngest of the four golf tournaments considered Majors, it is arguably the most significant because its founder was the legendary career-amateur Bobby Jones, and because it is played every year at the same golf course, Augusta National. As one of the most exclusive country clubs in the world, the Augusta National club has a long history of discrimination, and the ability to resist any attempts to change its policies. Leading up to the 2003 Masters, the president of the National Organization of Women, Martha Burk, challenged the officers of Augusta to admit its first woman member. Burk threatened to call a boycott of the companies sponsoring the tournament because of Augusta's discriminatory policies. Indicative of the financial clout of the club and its members, the club announced that it would sponsor the telecast itself and provided coverage without any commercial interruptions.

CBS first televised the tournament in 1956, and has retained the contract ever since. And while the network covets this perennial ratings leader, it has very little control over many of the aspects of the event, unlike most other tournament telecasts. The club dictates the number of commercials (no more than four per hour), and, whether directly or not, they have final say over the selection of announcers. There have been several situations when the club has flexed its muscles in this regard. During the 1994 telecast one of the commentators, Gary McCord, suggested that the greens had been "bikini- waxed" (the closer the greens are cut, the more difficult they are to putt). The following year Gary McCord was replaced for the Masters broadcast.

The Masters is different from the other Majors also in that the field is determined by invitation, and the invitations are determined by the Augusta members. This fact has contributed to the feeling among minorities that they have been systematically excluded from the Masters because of discrimination. The most bitter example of this is represented by black golfer Charlie Sifford. Sifford was one of the first black players to secure a PGA card and to win a tournament on the PGA Tour. During the period from 1961 to 1974 he was the only black golfer who played at a level that would qualify him to play in the Masters. Sifford described an incident in 1962 when he was leading the Canadian Open after the first round. Traditionally, a Masters invitation had gone automatically to the winner of the Canadian Open. At the conclusion of his round Siffird noticed someone had posted on the clubhouse bulletin board a note indicating that this year an invitation to the Masters would not be offered the Canadian Open winner.[47]

At one time the top 16 finishers at various tournaments would automatically get an invitation to the Masters. In 1960 at the U.S. Open, Sifford was in contention on the final day. The late sportswriter and commentator Dick Schaap related a conversation in *Sports Illustrated:*

> "If Charlie Sifford has a real hot round," a writer said, "he can finish among the top 16. Now that would be interesting. That would mean he would automatically qualify for the Masters tournament next year." "Y'all crazy?" said a reporter from Georgia. "If Sifford makes the top 16, they'll change the rules so only the top 15 qualify. If he finishes 11th, it'll be the top 10. And if he finishes second, then it'll be the top one."[48]

The top 25 money winners automatically got a Masters' invitation at one time. In 1967, Sifford had one of his best years and was high enough on the money list to be invited, however, the criteria were changed and a point system was devised to determine who would be invited. Not surprisingly for Sifford he did not have enough points to qualify.

Lee Elder is best known as the first black golfer to compete in the Masters in 1975. Throughout the early '70s Elder was the focal point of the effort to obtain equality in entrance to the Masters. By 1971 the Masters changed earlier policies which invited players on the basis of a complicated point system and by ballot of former Masters Champions. The new policy granted an invitation to anyone who won a PGA tournament in the year prior to the Masters.[49] In 1973, a group of 18 members of Congress, led by Representative Herman Badillo, sent a letter to Clifford Roberts, chairman of the Masters, urging that Lee Elder be invited to compete in the tournament.[50] Roberts refused the request. Elder himself rejected the idea and publicly responded, "There is only one [way] left for me to get into the Masters field this year, that's if I can win either at New Orleans or Greensboro. That's certainly what I'm going to try to do."[51] The following week Elder shot a 65 in the first round of the New Orleans Open and led by two strokes, but faltered and did not win. The following spring Elder won the Monsanto Open in Pensacola, Florida, and thus qualified for the 1975 Masters—the year Tiger Woods was born.

Tiger Woods faced none of the problems of Sifford and Elder as he prepared to play in his first Masters as a professional. By virtue of his victories on the tour and his place on the money list, Tiger had secured an invitation to the Masters, however by that time the public interest in Tiger Woods guaranteed him an invitation by any set of criteria.

With expectations running high at the Masters, Tiger Woods prepared to tee off with his fellow competitor, Nick Faldo, a three-time winner of the Masters and defending champion. It is a Masters' tradition that the defending champion be paired with the amateur champion, in this case Tiger Woods. Despite the fact that Tiger had turned professional since his amateur victory, the tradition was honored. It was apparent from Tiger's opening drive that he was not yet in his rhythm. He bogeyed the first hole and finished the first nine hole at four over par—40. Throughout the press corps, murmurs of over inflated expectations were prevalent. But suddenly on the 10th hole, Woods regained control of his game when he rolled in a birdie putt. Then in famous Amen Corner[52] he made a shot that maintained his momentum and probably saved the round and the tournament. He hit his tee shot to the par three 12th hole over the green and had a difficult chip shot to save par. He boldly chipped the ball into the hole for birdie and went on to shoot a near record-tying 30 on the back nine. At a score of 70, two under par, Tiger was only three shots behind the leader, John Huston.

Tiger played with Paul Azinger on the second day, and he was clearly more confident as he walked to the first tee. He had proven that he could put up a good score at Augusta. He proceeded to shoot a score that vaulted him into the lead. His 66 gave him a three-shot lead over Scotsman Colin Montgomerie. By the end of the third round he had increased the lead to nine shots. Colin Montgomerie had earlier in the season commented to the press that Tiger's reputation had been forged on what he referred to as "resort courses," and that he looked forward to facing Tiger at the Ryder Cup matches (a biannual competition between American professionals and European professionals) later in the fall. At his press conference after the third round at the Masters, Montgomerie was beside himself in describing the play of Woods: "I appreciate that he hit the ball long and straight, and I appreciate his iron shots were accurate. I do not appreciate how he putted. When you add it all together, he's nine shots clear, and I'm sure it will be higher tomorrow."[53]

The final round of the 1997 Masters had little to do with who would win the tournament. The previous year, Greg Norman, perennial contender for the Masters, held a six-shot lead over Nick Faldo at the start of the final round, and wound up losing by five strokes. The general wisdom is that the Masters doesn't really begin until the back nine on Sunday. The only question was whether the pressure would get to Woods. It didn't.

After playing even par for the first nine, he proceeded to birdie three holes on the back nine that had him standing on the 18th tee needing a par to break the 72-hole scoring record for the Masters. A photographer rapid-fired three quick shutter clicks at the top of Tiger's backswing, which caused him to pull his drive left onto the adjacent fairway. After sufficiently reprimanding the guilty party, he proceeded to hit the second shot on the green and calmly sunk a four-foot putt to break the record and win his first major championship.

This would be the first of many major championships but the significance of Tiger's win reverberated throughout the African American community. Lee Elder was invited to the final round and was at greenside when Woods sunk the last putt. Charlie Sifford rejoiced from his home in Kingston, Texas. This win was a vindication for all the African American players who had toiled to make a living playing golf...let alone playing in, or winning, the Masters Tournament. And beyond the social significance of Tiger's win at Augusta, this event had gained importance well beyond the golf community. The ratings for CBS's final round coverage were 15.8. This represented about 15.3 million television sets tuned to the Masters to watch this young black man play golf. That Sunday night only 60 Minutes had a higher rating, and the lead-in for that program was the Masters broadcast.

THE RECORDS

Over the next seven years Tiger Woods would compile a record that is unparalleled in the history of the sport. He entered 203 tournaments, worldwide, and finished 145 times in the top 10. He won 55 times and finished second in 23 tournaments. He won over $45 million in prize money. Among his many records accomplished on the PGA Tour, his run of six consecutive PGA tournaments in a row stands out. Starting with the PGA Championship on August 15, 1999, Tiger won six consecutive PGA tournaments ending with the AT&T Pebble Beach National Pro-

Am on January 9, 2000. During this streak, considerable attention was paid to the historical significance of Tiger's quest to replace the legendary figure, Byron Nelson, who in 1945 set the record, winning 11 consecutive tournaments. However, it should be noted that when Nelson set the record he was playing on a tour with relatively few full-time professionals. Consequently the depth of the competition could not be compared with the PGA Tour of 1999–2000, where virtually every player on the tour was a full-time tournament golfer. World War II was just ending, and the quality of the tour was further depleted because of the potential professionals who were in military service. For winning 11 tournaments, Nelson won $52,000, which has no comparison to the monumental purses on the modern PGA Tour. Finally, in 1945 the media exerted considerably less influence on the American public than the high-powered newspaper, magazine, radio, and international television coverage of contemporary tour events.

It looked to all that the streak would come to an end at the AT&T Invitational at Pebble Beach in early February as Tiger trailed by five shots going into the final round. On the 15th hole, he was still four shots behind the leader, Matt Gogel. Woods hit his approach shot to the par four hole and the ball bounced on the green, spun to the left and rolled into the hole for a rare eagle two. He trailed by two stokes. He birdied two of the final three holes and was declared the winner. When Tiger finally lost the next week to Phil Mickelsen in the 2000 Buick Invitational, he had tied the streak of Ben Hogan in 1948, when he won six consecutive PGA tournaments.

But while his record in regular tour events is impressive, it is Tiger's ability to win major tournaments that has separated him from any other golfer playing today. Sports writers had coined the term "Grand Slam" when Bobby Jones in 1930 won the U.S. Open and Amateur, and the British Open and Amateur. Since the two amateur championships became less important with the evolution of a legitimate professional tour, the writers invented a professional Grand Slam which included the U.S. and British Opens, the Masters, and the U.S. PGA Championship. Only five players, over their careers, ever won all four championships. At 24, Tiger Woods was the youngest player to achieve this feat. There are only five players in the history of the sport who have won all four tournaments during their career: Jack Nicklaus (age 26), Gary Player (age 29), Gene Sarazen (age 33), Ben Hogan (age 40), and Tiger. While the professional career Grand Slam had been done before, golfers and the press had only speculated on the possibility of a player winning all four tournaments in the same year.

Only one player had ever come close. Ben Hogan had a promising career in 1949 when he was injured in a near fatal automobile accident, after which doctors said he would never walk again, let alone play tournament golf. After tortuous rehabilitation and by virtue of his indomitable will, Hogan resumed a professional golf career. In 1953, at age 41, Hogan won five of six tournaments he entered, including three Majors: the Masters, the U.S. Open, and the British Open.[54] That's as close as anyone had come to winning pro golf's Grand Slam, the four majors in the same year, until Tiger Woods.

In 2000 the U.S. Open was held at Pebble Beach in California. Tiger Woods became the fifth person to lead the Open start to finish, and set a record for the lowest score in relation to par. The first of Tiger's two U.S. Open Championships, no one was even thinking about a Grand Slam with this victory.

Later that summer the British Open was conducted at the birthplace of golf and home of the Royal & Ancient Society, St. Andrews. Tiger shot 67 for the first round and was in second place. In the second round he scored 66. He had played 36 holes without a bogey. In the third round Tiger finally scored a bogey, but by the conclusion of the round he held a six-stroke lead over fellow American and friend David Duval. They were paired together on the last day. Duval got to within three strokes of Tiger on the front nine, but faltered on the 17th hole, when he took eight shots after failing to get out of the famous road hole bunker. Tiger finished with a 68 and his winning total, 19 under par, won by 8 strokes, which established a record for the British Open in relation to par. Suddenly the possibility of Tiger holding the four Major championships simultaneously, albeit over two seasons, was a possibility. The press was roughly divided on whether or not such a feat would be a true Grand Slam. The fact that there was even speculation that Tiger would be able to do it, let alone what it would be called, testifies to the monumental scale of his reputation.

The Vallhalla Golf Club in Louisville, Kentucky was the site for the final major of the year, the PGA Championship. Tiger opened with a 66 and followed with a 67 to lead by one stroke going into the weekend. On Saturday, Tiger birdied the final hole to maintain his one stroke lead over Bob May. May held the lead until the 17th hole when Tiger drew even. On the 18th hole, a par five, Tiger was forced to sink a curling six-foot putt to tie May and trigger a sudden-death playoff. On the third playoff hole, both Woods and May hit errant tee shots, and neither reached the green in two. Tiger hit a brilliant shot from a bunker short of the green, forcing May to make a long putt over an undulating green, which he missed by inches. Tiger was the PGA champion for the second year in a row.

Now the debate started in earnest. If Tiger was able to win the 2001 Masters the following April would it be a Grand Slam? He would hold all four championships within a calendar year—albeit not the same year. The press and the sports-minded public would have eight months to discuss it. The sports talk radio programs had a field day.

Tiger started slow in the first round of the Masters the following spring. He shot 67 but the course was ripe for low scores and he found himself five shots off the lead. On Friday he rebounded and shot a 66 to take a one shot lead on the field. On Saturday he maintained the one shot lead and set up another confrontation with his ever-present rivals David Duval and Phil Mickelsen. The three golfers battled throughout the Sunday round. By the 15th hole, Duval was tied with Woods, and Mickelsen was one stroke behind. Both Mickelsen and Duval bogeyed the critical 16th hole while Tiger parred. A definitive birdie putt on the 18th hole concluded the round for Tiger and assured his victory and claim to at least a form of a Grand Slam.

When asked if he considered this the Grand Slam at the press conference following the presentation ceremony, Tiger said that the press could call it whatever they wanted, but he had all four trophies in his possession at the same time. Ironically the debate over defining the feat overshadowed the sheer brilliance of it. Considering the immense amount of public attention focused on Tiger, the twelve months of building pressure, and the level of competition he faced, the Tiger Slam, as it came to be known, represents, to date, the single most exceptional accomplishment in modern golf history.

RYDER CUP COMPETITION

While Tiger has mounted an unprecedented record of accomplishment in individual events, he has not fared as well in the two major team-play competitions: The Ryder Cup Matches, and the relatively recent addition, the President's Cup Matches,[55] which pit the best American professionals against the best international players (excluding Europe).

The Ryder Cup is a competition that was initiated in 1927 when Samuel Ryder put up a trophy as a prize for the competition that would match American professionals against the best British professionals, alternating between the two countries. Ryder, an Englishman from St. Albans in Hertfordshire, made his fortune selling penny seed packets. Initially the press paid little attention to the matches since the American professionals dominated the competition until the 1960s. It wasn't until 1977 that the British team was expanded to include European players, a move intended to upgrade the Ryder Cup competitive level, that the event started to attract an audience. The U.S. had won all but one match from 1959 to 1977, that being tied, 16 to 16, in a memorable duel in 1969 at Royal Birkdale in Southport, England.

Since the British team was expanded to include all European players, the matches have become much more competitive and took on importance both in Europe and in America. Of the last nine matches the American team has won only three. In addition to the inclusion of all European countries, several factors have contributed to this reversal. The European tour is less affluent than the American tour, and American pros tend to travel alone and stay alone on the road. The European tour is also smaller and the players tend to socialize together more than in American professional golf. Since members of the European team tend to be less-recognized players, they have more to prove than the star-filled American team. In part because of Tiger's outstanding amateur record in match play tournaments, and the tremendous amount of publicity his debut on the PGA Tour had generated, expectations were high that Tiger's presence would significantly enhance the American's chances of winning.

The Ryder Cup competition consists of a three-day event alternating every two years between America and Europe. It starts on Friday when there are five matches in the morning. Two players on each team do not compete, so the Captains must determine who will play and the order of the matches. The format is called foursomes, in which the players alternate shots, using one ball. The team with the lowest score on a hole wins that hole. The team that wins the most holes wins the match. When one team has won more holes than there are remaining, they win the match. The winning team gets a point. If the teams tie, a half point is awarded.

The afternoon matches play a "four ball" format. This is the most common form of competition among recreational golfers. In it, each player plays his own ball. The lowest score of one team is compared to the lowest score of the other team, to determine the winner of that hole. The team that wins the most holes wins the match. On Sunday there are 12 individual matches, involving the entire team. There are potentially 32 points to be won. So to win the Ryder Cup a team must win at least 16½ points. If a tie occurs, the team currently holding the cup retains it.

Tiger Woods has competed in four Ryder Cup matches since joining the professional tour. His overall record in those matches is 7 wins, 11 losses and 2 ties. It should be noted that he has fared better in the singles matches than in the team play, but overall the American team has only won once with him on the team. There has been considerable speculation as to why he has not dominated the Ryder Cup like all other competitions he has attempted. While it is impossible to pinpoint the reason for his less-than-outstanding performance in the Ryder Cup, there have been several incidents relating to the Ryder Cup that highlight an aspect of Tiger's career which has evolved as his golfing reputation has grown: the higher his celebrity profile, the more the press and the public have expected him to speak out on issues.

In 1997 the PGA, which conducted the Ryder Cup matches, would not pay for Earl Woods to accompany Tiger to the matches in Vallderama, Spain, a perk afforded the wives of married players on the team. At the time, Tiger commented on the logic of this policy. Then several months before the matches in 1999, to be held at the Country Club in Brookline, Massachusetts, David Duval was quoted in a *Golf Digest* article complaining about what he called the hypocrisy of the Ryder Cup. Players were not paid to compete on the team. Only their expenses were paid. Duval complained that since the PGA made a considerable overall profit on the matches ($23.5 million according to the article),[56] and the players put their reputations on the line at these matches, he thought that there should be some compensation for the players, even if it was in the form of a contribution to the charity of the player's choice.

Even though many players had privately voiced similar concerns, Tiger was the only member of the team who spoke up publicly in support of Duval. At a press conference at the PGA Championship at Medinah, outside of Chicago, Tiger agreed with Duval that the players should derive more benefits from playing in these matches. The subsequent furor over his remarks, as the media generally sided with golf's establishment, in this case the PGA of America and the PGA Tour. Eventually the PGA acquiesced and devised a plan whereby the players would have the right to donate a certain amount of money to a charity. However, this incident represents the pressures confronting Tiger Woods once he established his position as the number-one golfer in the world. It would not be the only one.

NOTES

1. United States Golf Association, "USGA History," http://www.usga.org/aboutus/usga_history/usga_history.html.

2. Mark Frost, *The Greatest Game Ever Played* (New York: Hyperion, 2002), 107–108.

3. Mark Frost, *Grand Slam: Bobby Jones, America, and the Story of Golf* (New York: Hyperion Books) 17.

4. Atlanta History Center, "Down the Fairway with Bobby Jones," http://www.bobbyjonesgolfexhibit.com/Timeline/main_timeline.html..

5. John Feinstein, *The Majors* (Boston: Little, Brown and Company, 1999), 13–14.

6. The term refers to the early custom of awarding a medal to the winner of the amateur competitions. In medal competition the player with the fewest number of strokes during the entire round wins.

7. The term is generally considered to be from the French verb *dormir*—to sleep. In essence, the player would have to fall asleep to lose the match.

8. John Strege, *A Biography of Tiger Woods* (New York: Broadway Books, 1998), 69–70.

9. Quoted in Strege, 71.

10. Quoted in ibid., 123.

11. Ibid., 126.

12. Ibid., 168.

13. Ibid., 174.

14. The Mid-Amateur Championship was created in 1981 for amateurs over 25 years old.

15. Ibid., 176.

16. Joe Drape, "New Study Shows Gap on Court and in Class," *New York Times*, 16 March 2005, D5.

17. Strege, 81.

18. U.S. Department of Justice, "Faces of the ADA—Casey Martin continues his professional golf career. 17 July 2000, http://www.usdoj.gov/crt/ada/fmartin.htm.

19. PGA Tour, "Notah Begay-Media Guide," http://www.pgatour.com/players/bio/149683

20. Quoted in Strege, 82.

21. As quoted in Strege, 83.

22. Nicholas Edwards, *Tiger Woods: An American Master* (New York: Scholastic Inc. 1997), 136.

23. Strege, 88–89.

24. John Strege, 135.

25. Earl Woods, *Playing Through* (New York: Harper Collins, 1998), 122.

26. Quoted in Strege, 85.

27. Woods, 128–129.

28. Ibid., 133.

29. Strege, 157–160.

30. Woods, 141–152.

31. Quoted in Strege, 188.

32. Ibid., 189.

33. Ibid., 194.

34. Ibid., 191.

35. Quoted in Tim Roseforte, 91.

36. Quoted in Strege, 192.

37. Roseforte, 64.

38. John Feinstein, *The First Coming* (New York: Ballantine), 10.

39. Quoted in Strege, 194.

40. Frost, *Grand Slam*, 99.

41. Roseforte, 72.

42. Quoted in Strege, 202.

43. Strege, 212.

44. Roseforte, 92.

45. Strege, 216.

46. Quoted in Roseforte, 100.

47. Quoted in Charlie Sifford, *Just Let Me Play*, (New York: British American Publishing), 175.

48. Ibid., 176.

49. "Masters Policy Change Seen as Aid to Blacks," *New York Times,* 13 June 1971, sec V: 5.

50. Lincoln A. Werden, "18 in House Demand Masters Invite Black Golfer," *New York Times,* 18 March 1973: 1.

51. Lincoln A. Werden, "Special-Bid Idea Disliked by Elder," *New York Times,* 20 March 1973: 45.

52. So named because of the abrupt change of the hole directions and the difficulties of the 11th through 13th holes, often forcing players to rely on divine intervention.

53. Quoted in Rosaforte, 127.

54. This was the only time Hogan played in the British Open. The PGA Championship in 1953 was scheduled during the British Open, thus making it impossible for Hogan to even attempt the Grand Slam.

55. The Presidents Cup was initiated in 1994. It is a three-day series of matches featuring professionals from the U.S. against international players (excluding Europe).

56. Rosaforte, 152.

Chapter 6

IMPACT

There is no question that during his short career Tiger Woods has had a significant impact on the game of golf and the PGA Tour. However, his life so far has had influence beyond the realm of sports. While he is certainly not the first athlete or celebrity to endorse consumer products, the scale of his compensation and variety of products he endorses have ramped up the standards within the advertising industry. As a minority celebrity he is expected by some to not only excel on the field but also represent the interests of all minorities on issues that have nothing to do with sports. It is impossible to separate his growing celebrity from the media-saturated environment we occupy. Without the media—especially broadcast television—there would not be a Tiger Woods phenomenon.

SPORTS AND BROADCASTING

The first regularly licensed commercial radio station is generally considered to be KDKA, which began broadcasting on November 2, 1920.[1] Within six months the first sports broadcast occurred on KDKA when Florent Gibson, a sportswriter for the *Pittsburgh Post* was enlisted to provide what we now call a blow-by-blow description of a prize fight on April 11, 1921. The station began broadcasting the Pittsburgh Pirate baseball games on August 5, 1921. The marriage of sports and broadcasting grew out of the broadcasters' desperate need for programming once they went on the air. They needed programming that didn't cost much and had some mass appeal. Sports provided the perfect solution to their problem. In the early days of this relationship, sports team owners were wary of this new technology, but since there weren't enough receivers to have much impact, they didn't object.

As the number of listeners grew, team owners began to worry that prospective customers, who would normally attend games and pay for tickets, would stay at home and listen to the game on the radio for free. So immediately the question of the value of rights for a particular sporting event had to be settled. Several court cases eventually confirmed that sports teams owned the rights to their games. In one case a team wouldn't allow the broadcast of its games, so the broadcasters, KGHI in Little Rock, Arkansas, erected a platform in a tree a few hundred feet from the stadium, hooked up a telephone line and began describing the game over the air. In 1934 the local court told the station to get out of the tree. The federal courts further confirmed the principle in 1938 when KQV in Pittsburgh was sued for recreating Pirates games,[2] stolen from two stations that had paid for broadcast rights. The stations were joined in the suit by the sponsors of the legal broadcast, since by this time the idea of selling advertisements to sponsors to underwrite the cost of production and make a profit was firmly entrenched.

On April 30, 1939, a television broadcast from New York City featured President Franklin D. Roosevelt opening the World's Fair. The broadcast was carried on the National Broadcasting Company (NBC), which had established the first station to provide sporadic television programming to a few receivers owned mainly by NBC executives. Less than a month later, on May 17, NBC broadcast the first television coverage of a sporting event, a baseball game between Columbia University and Princeton University.[3] The coverage was limited as they used only one camera for the game and interviews. World War II significantly slowed down the evolution of commercial television as virtually all research and development was dedicated to the war effort, and after the war the Federal Communications Commission (FCC) imposed a two-year freeze on the issuance of any new licenses. The Nielsen Media Research Company found a jump in television households from 9 percent in 1949 to 64.5 percent in 1954.[4] Television was firmly established as a principal means of providing information and entertainment to the American public.

Just as with radio, sports provided television a staple programming product which attracted a mass audience and cost relatively little to produce. In the early days, boxing was the easiest sport to broadcast, and consequently it dominated early television schedules. It took place indoors in a relatively small area, and was able to be covered with very few cameras, hence low production costs. As it was not seasonal, the sport was a natural for television. The DuMont television network was the first network to televise boxing, along with a number of other firsts in broadcasting, including the first professional football game and the first daytime drama (or soap opera). Early on baseball became by far the most popular televised sport—especially the World Series. In 1947 NBC televised the first World Series, and fortunately for the network the two competing teams were both from New York,[5] as was the case when NBC made the first radio broadcast of a World Series 26 years earlier.[6]

The appeal of broadcast golf took much longer to catch on. In 1938, Dave Garroway, who would later gain fame as the avuncular host of NBC's *Today* television morning show, carried a bulky remote radio transmitter on his back as he competed in a celebrity golf tournament. He reported on his stroke-by-stroke progress for his audience listening on KDKA. The unwieldy equipment hempered his swing and he played poorly, but fortunately for Garroway there is no record of his score.[7] As has been stated earlier, golf at this time was not a sport for the masses, and attracted little attention from a mass audience. It wasn't until the election of Dwight Eisenhower to the American presidency in 1952 that the game began to gain wider appeal.

Eisenhower, the popular leader of the Allied Forces during World War II, was an avid golfer and was responsible for popularizing the sport beyond the country club set. He played golf regularly and even had a putting green installed on the White House lawn and practiced occasionally between meetings. He was a member of Augusta National Golf Club, home of the Masters and Bobby Jones, and undoubtedly his membership called attention to the annual playing of the Masters.

In the late 1950s there was an explosion of golf coverage on television. In addition to the influence Eisenhower, remote television equipment became smaller and made it possible to televise an event over a five-acre playing field with action occurring simultaneously. There was also more money to spend on leisure during this period and more people were playing golf. Though the ratings for televised golf have never approached the level of the big three television sports—baseball, football and basketball—sponsors eagerly buy advertising in golf tournaments. Even though the audience for golf is relatively small in comparison to the big three television sports, it is a demographic that is coveted by advertisers: people who are interested in upscale products like luxury automobiles, business systems, investment companies, travel, and the golf equipment the pros use. Interestingly golf delivers 35 percent more voters than an evening network news broadcast.[8]

But by far the most important factor in popularizing the game of golf was the arrival of Arnold Palmer as the most popular and telegenic personality in golf before Tiger Woods. Palmer, the son of a golf professional, was born and raised in Latrobe, Pennsylvania. His father, Milfred J. "Deacon" Palmer, worked at the Latrobe Country Club as the golf professional and course superintendent. However, Palmer didn't enjoy a country club upbringing. He was solidly blue-collar and worked hard for his father on the course; along the way he developed a strong golf game. He possessed rugged good looks and had the kind of flair that just lent itself to television. He withdrew from Wake Forest University during his senior year and, after serving a three-year tour in the Coast Guard, he won the 1954 U.S. Amateur Championship. He met and married Winifred "Winnie" Walzer, and embarked on a career as a professional golfer.

At a time when golfers, as professional athletes, were generally considered dull, Palmer was a revelation. In a game that was perceived as boring by all except those who played it, Palmer brought a new element that made golf tournaments exciting. He didn't just *win* tournaments, he charged out and overwhelmed them. With the ability to cover multiple holes simultaneously, and to be up close and personal, television amplified Palmer's style of play. He began to win tournaments, usually coming from several strokes behind on the last few holes—the media began to call it a "charge." Legend has it that during one of his charges at an early Masters, one of the uniformed soldiers from the nearby Ft. Gordon (then Camp Gordon) Army post who were manning scoreboards raised a sign that said "Arnie's Army" and that's what the television commentators started calling Palmer's fans. It stuck. Palmer and the Masters would be forever linked.[9]

The first Masters was televised in 1956. While Palmer was not a factor, Jackie Burke made up eight strokes on the final day to overtake amateur Ken Venturi by one stroke. In 1958 Palmer won his first major championship at Augusta. A situation occurred on the 12th hole; Palmer's ball embedded in a bank behind the green. Due to heavy rain the night before, a local rule was in effect that allowed players to lift and drop embedded balls, but the official on the hole wasn't sure if the rule was applicable where Palmer's ball was embedded. He informed Palmer that he could play the ball as it lay, and play a second ball (also allowed under the Rules of Golf). Palmer made a five with the first ball and a three with the second ball. Three holes later, after he holed a long putt for an eagle, Palmer was informed that the second ball counted. He defeated Ken Venturi by one stroke. In 2004 Venturi revisited the 1958 Masters incident when he raised a controversy in his autobiography, *Getting Up & Down: My 60 Years in Golf*, where he stated that Palmer had violated a rule when he didn't announce that he intended to play the second ball until he scored double bogey with the first. Irrespective of the intricacies of the Rules of Golf, the interest in Palmer and golf was growing to a larger and more diverse national television audience.

Palmer needed to birdie the final two holes of the 1960 Masters to once again defeat Ken Venturi by one stroke. Winning his fifth tournament for the year, Palmer made a 30-foot putt on the 17th hole and a six-foot putt on the 18th hole. Two years later, Palmer participated in the first three-way playoff with Gary Player and Dow Finsterwald, winning by three strokes for his third Masters title. In 1964, Palmer, after tying for the first round leading the remaining three rounds to win by six strokes, won his last Masters Championship and in doing so became the first player to win four Masters.[10] Palmer's exposure on the PGA Tour, especially in the Masters, which garnered exceptionally high television ratings for any program, let alone the sport of golf, led to many business opportunities beyond the golf course.

Between his discharge from the Coast Guard in 1954 and the start of his professional golf career, Palmer worked as a salesman in Cleveland, where he had been stationed. During that time he became reacquainted with a young lawyer he met when he competed in college golf. Mark McCormack graduated from Duke University and began working for the Cleveland law firm Arter, Hadden, Wykoff and Van Durzer. That relationship developed into one of the most lucrative business arrangements in sports, and led to the start of an industry.

THE MARKETING OF TIGER WOODS

Palmer was not the first sports star to endorse products. As early as 1905 Honus Wagner, "The Flying Dutchman," signed a contract giving J. F. Hillerich & Son permission to use his autograph on Louisville Slugger bats. Not only was Wagner the first of countless baseball stars to sign a contract with the Hillerichs, but he was the first known professional athlete to endorse a retail product. Perhaps the greatest baseball player of all time, Ty Cobb, signed a contract with J. F. Hillerich & Son for autographed Louisville Slugger bats in 1906.[11]

When Arnold Palmer began on the PGA Tour, most of the extra money he or any other pro made beyond prize money was from exhibition matches that were usually played on the Monday before the tournament began later in the week. In 1958 Palmer asked Mark McCormack and his partner Dick Taylor to act as his representative to make the arrangements for these matches. That year McCormack formed National Sports Management and represented Palmer and golfer Dow Finsterwald. The following year Palmer asked McCormack to represent him in all his business matters and thus McCormack became the first sports agent.[12] National Sports Management soon became International Management Group (IMG).

IMG has since evolved into a multinational corporation with clients well beyond the sports world.[13] The firm represents celebrities, mostly athletes, and in addition has become involved in actually running events that are created so that their clients will have a platform on which to perform and earn money—which in turn earns commission money for IMG. The company has expanded into virtually every facet of the entertainment industry. An example of the extent to which the tentacles of IMG reach is a deal where, "The writer of a book agented by IMG Literary and printed and distributed by IMG Publishing interviewing golfers who are IMG clients at an IMG-created golf tournament for which they receive appearance fees from the tournament organizer—IMG. The agency earns fees from sponsors, and sells the television rights, and God knows what else."[14]

It was Mark McCormack, through IMG, who originated the idea of world rankings of golfers, thus internationalizing professional golf. Recently IMG expanded its interest in developing junior sports talents when it bought Nick Bollettieri's tennis camp in Bradenton, Florida and converted it into IMG Academies, where precocious young athletes, with well-off parents pay hefty tuitions in the hopes of college scholarships, if not a professional career. Many of the parents purchase $310,000 condominiums and live on the IMG campus with their kids.[15]

In 1960 Jack Nicklaus won the U.S. Open and also became a client of IMG. Both Palmer and Nicklaus represent a model that was the standard for athletes until Tiger Woods. Eventually IMG was representing Arnold Palmer, Jack Nicklaus, and Gary Player, the South African golfer who, along with Nicklaus, was to become one of the five golfers to have won the four major championships. These three players represented the most sought-after players on the tour and commanded the highest appearance fees. But their fees in comparison to those received today by Tiger Woods were small.

The image that IMG was trying to foster for their clients was one of success beyond the tournaments they won, and the products they endorsed reflected that success. However, in 1960 their clients had to rely on many, relatively small endorsements. These athletes had to continue working, and while IMG clients were wealthy, they had to invest their own money to create more wealth. Both Palmer and Nicklaus had several investment deals that were unsuccessful. Palmer invested in a network of Cadillac automobile dealerships that eventually had to be sold off at a loss. Similarly, Nicklaus had various ups and downs in his various business ventures.

There are other factors that balance the comparison between the commercial potential of today's celebrity athletes and early IMG clients. The change in the social climate has helped increase the potential market appeal for Tiger and his contemporaries. Compared to the early days of the civil rights movement in 1960 America, today's virtually universal acceptance of multiculturalism expands the commercial possibilities for a young athlete, particularly of mixed racial background. Finally, the performance of today's athletes is clearly superior to that in the days of Palmer and Nicklaus.

While there is no question that Palmer and Nicklaus pioneered the concept of sports marketing, the marketing of Tiger Woods reflects the change in the business climate for successful athletes. He averages about $10 million per endorsement deal, and more importantly rarely invests his own money. The difference between the cultural climate in 1960 and today is significant. The saturation of media now is overwhelming compared to the early 60s; there are more outlets and many more opportunities for synergies—the magic concept that drives corporations, particularly in media, to buy up parallel businesses and cross-promote their products at reduced costs. So it's not mere coincidence that a network television morning show does multiple stories about a movie produced by their parent or sister company. Modern advertising campaigns are built on product branding: if the product brand matches the athlete's so-called brand, the campaign is successful. Nike had assembled the outstanding performer in basketball (Michael Jordan), soccer (Mia Hamm), track (Michael Johnson), and now golf (Tiger Woods).

Despite the universal acceptance of advertising there is the ongoing question as to whether or not the advertising money spent is reflected in the sales of products. In August 1996, Nike stock sold for $35 per share; it soared to $75 per share at the peak of Tigermania; and dropped back to $35 per share in 2001. How much Tiger had to do with those numbers is not clear. The value of celebrity endorsement is an inexact science. Professor Russ Ackoff from the Wharton School at the University of Pennsylvania conducted an exhaustive study to determine which factors influenced the purchase of beer, and concluded the most reliable determinant was the weather; the hotter it got, the more beer people bought.[16] Scientific evidence to the contrary, advertisers were eager to attach their products to Tiger Woods.

The road to that attachment was through IMG agent Hughes Norton. A Harvard and Yale graduate, Norton joined IMG in 1972 and after an initially solid relationship with IMG client Greg Norman soured he rescued his career by convincing Earl and Tiger Woods to sign with IMG. He had begun to court the Woods family early on and was responsible for hiring Earl to act as a scout for IMG early in Tiger's junior career. There has been inevitable speculation about Norton's motives, but there was little doubt that Tiger would become an IMG client. There have been a number of situations where the press has been critical of Norton's handling of Tiger's affairs, particularly early in his career.

John Feinstein is a respected writer and media commentator who early on was critical in articles and interviews of Earl Woods and the handling of Tiger by IMG. He wrote that he thought IMG would, in a rush to capitalize on Tiger's instant fame, overschedule him with corporate outings and various other nontournament events. He warned that Tiger should be left to concentrate on winning golf tournaments rather than pile up endorsement money and corporate commitments. But when he compared Earl Woods to Stefano Capriati, the quintessential sports parent, whose daughter, Jennifer had burned out after a brilliant start in tennis, Feinstein was effectively banished by Team Tiger.

At about this time IMG was considering which golf magazine Tiger should affiliate with as a playing editor, *Golf Digest* or *Golf World*. Feinstein wrote for *Golf World* and his editor, George Peper, arranged for a meeting with Norton to try and clear the air and possibly give his magazine a chance at securing the services of the young professional golfer. Norton implied that if Feinstein would be less critical of Tiger and Earl they would consider seriously *Golf World* as Tiger's magazine home. Feinstein announced that if his writing was toned down by editors he would quit. That didn't happen and Tiger signed on with *Golf Digest*. If there was any doubt, it was very clear how Norton would represent his new client.[17] Whether incidents like this were examples of mismanagement, or the product of normal interpersonal conflict and misunderstanding present in any business transaction, by 2000, with Earl's health deteriorating, Tiger was beginning to call his own shots. That wasn't the case when the first Nike campaign was conceived.

The idea for the Nike Company grew out of a term paper by Phil Knight, speculating on the creation of a company that would sell running shoes. Knight was a runner at the University of Oregon under track coach Bill Bowerman, whose protégé would later be distance runner Steve Prefontaine, who died of cancer. Knight's interest in Tiger was fuelled when the young star won his third U.S. Junior Amateur at the Waverly

Country Club, which was Knight's home course in Oregon. Nike was one of the first new age companies. Its headquarters in Beaverton, Oregon is called a campus because "Isn't everybody a college junior at heart?"[18] In addition to offices it features dry cleaners, a gym, barber shops, and a cafeteria with scales to weigh your sliced turkey.

This was the company that designed the campaign that produced the television spot that featured Tiger talking directly to the camera: "There are still courses in the U.S. that I am not allowed to play because of the color of my skin. Hello, World. I've heard I'm not ready for you. Are you ready for me?"[19] The commercial immediately caused an uproar within the golf community and the press. Columnist James K. Glassman of the *Washington Post* questioned in a column exactly which courses Tiger would not be able to play. David Faye, the Executive Director of the USGA, contacted Nike to point out that the golf shirt Tiger was wearing in the commercial had the logo of Butch Harmon's home course, Lochinvar Golf Club in Houston, which did not allow women members.[20] The general consensus was that the theme of the ad was somewhat disingenuous. Granted there were golf courses in America where African Americans could not play, but they certainly did not exclude Tiger Woods. Critics questioned why, after not concentrating on his color before the campaign—he had in fact asked that reporters refer to him not as African American or Asian, but as an American—race was suddenly a primary issue. Tiger responded to questions indicating that he had approved the copy, and that he wanted the message of the commercial to stoke controversy and get people talking about the issue, and he added that while he no longer is the target of discrimination, when he was growing up he was. Finally, some golf traditionalists felt uncomfortable with the in-your-face style of the spot, which conjured up images of urban macho rather than country club golf chic. There is little question that, regardless of the appropriateness of this spot, the reaction to the golf community represented a clear example of the ambiguity it was feeling toward this new personality. There was more to come.

Whether planned or not, the "Are You Ready for Me?" campaign quickly disappeared from the airwaves, and was replaced by a softer Tiger image. The ad featured a series of shots of children of various ethnicities identifying themselves as Tiger Woods. The clear message: Tiger represents all people. Once again the ad sparked controversy. Most of the criticism by the press centered more on Nike, and the fact that Tiger Woods was being manipulated by the corporate image makers, than on the golfer himself. Nonetheless, the initial attempts to define the public persona of this new star were tentative at best.

By far the most successful ad produced early in Tiger's career was the one in which he ad-libbed remarks while bouncing a golf ball off the face of a club while talking to the camera. He performs a series of tricks while bouncing the ball, and finally bounces the ball above his head and just before it strikes the ground takes a full swing and drives it down the fairway. Commentators speculated whether the commercial involved special editing effects, but it subsequently came out that Tiger was able to accomplish the feat on only the fifth take while filming. He explained to kids during a golf clinic later that he developed the technique while waiting on the usually crowded tees at the par-three golf course he grew up on, Heartwell, back in California.[21]

During these initial campaigns, the by-now famous Nike logo was in evidence in virtually every frame of film and photograph. Nike had become aware of the possible dangers of oversaturation of their logo, especially in light of the fact that the company had been the target of criticism about the working conditions of foreign workers who actually made their products. They were starting to get comments from focus groups that referred to their ubiquitous logo as a "swooshstika."[22] Consequently they began developing individualized logos for some of their superstar endorsers, like Michael Jordan, who was identified with a jumping man symbol. In Tiger's case, they developed a stylized logo that merged his TW initials, and began to replace the Nike swoosh.

A good example of how important product endorsement is in sports marketing is Tiger's association with the Titleist company. Titleist manufactures the largest-selling golf ball. One of the main reasons for this is that more top golf professionals use Titleist than any other golf ball. Consequently more good amateur golfers and recreational golfers use Titleist's ProV1 golf ball. Player endorsement in golf marketing is serious business, unlike most other sports. In golf, even recreational players have the opportunity to play on the same golf courses as the professionals, and use the same equipment. It would be like a NASCAR fan getting the opportunity to take a lap at the Daytona Speedway, in a professional stockcar. So when a particular golf ball is used by most of the winning professionals, recreational golfers can purchase that ball to play their weekend games. Through the Tour Championships in November 2004, winners of 152 tournaments worldwide used Titleist gold balls, nearly 100 more than the nearest competitor. Consumers clearly took notice.[23]

So when Tiger turned pro and signed on with Titleist to use their golf balls, wear a Titleist golf glove and use a Titleist bag, for which he would be paid $3 million for three years,[24] the company benefited every time he teed up their ball in competition. However, in 2000, partly because of

Tiger's overwhelming successes, Nike began to manufacture golf equipment, notably their own golf balls. Actually, Nike doesn't manufacture
golf balls; Bridgestone in Japan and Wilson in the United States make
golf balls for Nike. Titleist was concerned that, since Nike was now in
the golf ball business, it would lead consumers to think Tiger was using a
Nike golf ball in his many successful Nike commercials. They sued and as
a result restructured their deal with the superstar, paying him only when
he used their ball in a tournament. Soon Tiger switched to the Nike ball,
and eventually began using Nike clubs as well. The competition became
so heated that Nike produced a commercial with Tiger in which he
described his contract with them that stipulated that he could use whatever equipment he chose, intended to show at once confidence in their
products, and the stature of Tiger to be able to warrant such liberty. In
2003 this liberty was exercised when Tiger announced that he was going
back to his Titleist driver.

Another initial corporate relationship arranged for Tiger by IMG was
with the American Express Company. Tiger represented the ideal spokesman for the financial institution. In one television ad we see Tiger playing golf in an urban landscape, negotiating obstacles to reach his goal,
with the somewhat belabored implication that AmEx cardholders will
be able to overcome the same obstacles. Despite the surrealistic style of
the commercials, the connection between Tiger and the good life was
made.[25] Tiger's relationship with American Express points out another
area of potential conflict with competing sponsors on the PGA Tour.
Tiger only competed once in the MasterCard Colonial Tournament, in
1997. In subsequent years he chose to play in the Deutsche Bank German
Open in Europe. Not coincidentally, this tournament was run by IMG,
and Tiger received appearance money for his efforts. Paying players to
compete in your tournament is allowed in Europe, but not on the PGA
Tour. Similarly, Tiger took exception with promotional material for the
2001 Mercedes Championship, after he won the 2000 event. There was
some concern that consumers might conclude that Tiger actually drove a
Mercedes rather than his corporate sponsor Buick.[26]

Nowhere in advertising is product branding more important than
automobiles. So it was surprising to advertising-industry observers that
Tiger wound up endorsing a Buick, a modest car aimed at a middle-class
consumer, rather than a Ferrari or Lamborghini. The general rule is that
a celebrity cannot improve their image after developing an association
with a down-scale brand. Fellow professional Fuzzy Zoeller had become
the spokesman for K-Mart earlier and had never really risen above the so-
called bargain image. Zoeller suffered severe criticism from PGA club pros

who make a living selling brand-name golf clubs, and who didn't want consumers getting the idea that you could buy clubs without the advice of a golf professional.[27] But the strong market appeal of Tiger Woods has defied all the general rules of marketing.

His appeal derives from a number of factors that converged to make Tiger Woods a marketing bonanza. He's young in a culture that idolizes youth. Nobody has accomplished what he has done in golf at his age. Consequently he is able to appeal to a coveted demographic while also reaching teenager's parents. He is strikingly good-looking. His combined genetic makeup produces a broad range of appeal that is not limited to one segment of the population. The fact that an African American has been able to succeed in a sport that has a long history of discrimination, at a time when racial discrimination is universally denounced, only reinforces the popularity of his accomplishments. Finally, his Asian mother has both physically and spiritually influenced Tiger to respect her Thai roots, and he has endeavored to play golf around the world. His presence has contributed to the overall evolution of golf as an international sport. Starting with the institution of the Sony World Rankings of golf professionals , the game has steadily grown as an international attraction. With the creation of the Golf Channel in 1980, international golf has become a regular feature in American homes. Interest in the Ryder Cup competition has also spawned the President's Cup, further fueling interest in international competition. Tiger Woods has been a contributing factor to this increased interest, while he has benefited financially as well.

BEING TIGER WOODS

Being Tiger Woods is certainly not without its challenges. Early on he and his original team experienced problems establishing his image. The fact that he had a team was a problem in itself. Before Tiger was a teenager, there was a group of people who, along with his parents, provided support for the budding superstar. Irrespective of who these people were and how much they contributed, his parents were always the final authority—especially Earl Woods. In addition to Earl and Kultida, the original team consisted of Hughes Norton, Butch Harmon, Fluff Cowan, Jay Brunza, and John Merchant. Since turning professional the team has not remained the same.

The most significant change in Tiger's advisors was Mark Steinberg, who replaced Hughes Norton as Tiger's IMG agent at the end of 1999. Steinberg was young, 30, and had a background in athletics. He was a backup player for the University of Illinois and sat on the bench during the 1989 NCAA Championships. Replacing Norton was a delicate situation. Norton, who had initially convinced Earl to consider signing up with IMG during Tiger's junior career, and arranged for Earl to work for IMG. There had been growing discontent with Hughes' over-scheduling Tiger in nontournament activities, which paid off in dollars (and commissions) but took their toll on the golfer.[28]

Claude "Butch" Harmon Jr. was the son of Claude Harmon, who defeated Dr. Cary Middlecoff by five strokes in the 1948 Masters. Claude was the father of four sons, all of whom were great teachers of golf; none of them could beat their father. After attending the University of Houston, for one year, Butch dropped out and joined the army. He served in Alaska where he won the Alaska State Amateur, and eventually spent six months in Vietnam. He competed for two years on the PGA Tour, and then went to Morocco, where he was King Hassan II's personal golf professional. It was at the Champions Club in Houston, after Tiger had lost in the second round of the 1993 US Amateur that Earl Woods had lunch with Harmon and asked if he would work with Tiger. Harmon was Tiger's coach from then until 2004.[29]

Throughout most of Tiger's junior career, navy psychiatrist Jay Brunza served as Tiger's caddie and sports psychologist. He was replaced on Tiger's bag at the 1996 US Amateur by Byron Bell. Brunza held no grudges, saying that "I trust Tiger's judgment about what he needs to win."[30]

When Tiger announced he was turning professional in 1996, Mike "Fluff" Cowan was his caddie. Cowan was loaned to Tiger by Peter Jacobson, who was recovering from a back injury. Eventually Fluff stayed on and some in the golf community felt that this was a breach of professional etiquette. Nonetheless, Cowan established a persona for himself with the media. He did his own commercials and was generally media friendly. By the 1999 Nissan Open, Tiger told Cowan that he was replacing him on his bag temporarily. Reportedly the reason was the overexposure Cowan was receiving in the media. In a *Golf Digest* interview Cowan disclosed his pay scale saying he "...made $1,000 a week, plus standard percentages for wins [10%] and top ten finishes,"[31] and finally when Tiger observed him doing television interviews, he was replaced.

Tiger's new caddie was in many ways the antithesis of Fluff. A New Zealander, fit and not at all conversant with the media, Steve Williams was working for Raymond Floyd when Tiger contacted him. He carried Tiger's bag for the first time at the 1999 Bay Hill Invitational in Florida in March. Tall, trim and athletic, a fairly accomplished golfer on his own, Williams often played practice rounds with Tiger. Where Fluff enjoyed interacting with the fans and the press, Williams was nowhere to be found after the round. And there was little chance of seeing Williams in any television commercials.

John Merchant was the first African American to be named to the USGA Executive Committee, and was involved in some of the decisions concerning Tiger's amateur status during his amateur career. A Connecticut lawyer, Merchant had worked with Earl in the mid-'90s in an organization called the National Minority Golf Foundation.[32] This group met annually and tried to encourage the growth of golf in the minority community. Several corporations helped underwrite the organization, including *Golf Digest* and Titleist. At one time Merchant served as the first head of the Tiger Woods Foundation. But in December of 1996 he was fired. Tiger has said he made the decision but Merchant says he was fired by Earl, "I haven't talked to Tiger since. I was puzzled by it. But lawyers come and go, so I got out of Dodge."[33]

Another new member of Team Tiger was Greg McLaughlin. Earl and Tiger had first encountered McLaughlin when he was a tournament director and granted sponsor's exemptions for Tiger at the 1991 Nissan Open and the Honda Classic in 1992. Later he served as director of the Western Golf Association. Indicative of Tiger's increasing assumption of control of his own affairs, McLaughlin commented, "I see a huge difference [in attitude] between 1997 and 1999. The swing changes are one thing, but he seems to be much more 'with it.' He manages the whole thing a lot better now than he did a couple of years ago. That comes with experience, age, maturity, whatever you want to call it."[34]

As he matured and his career flourished, the public wanted more information about Tiger and his personal life. The first public relationship with a woman became evident when Joanna Jagoda began attending Tiger's tournaments occasionally with Kultida. Jagoda was a former college cheerleader who went on to law school at Pepperdine University, and she fit the physical stereotype for the women of most touring professionals—tall, blonde, and attractive. At the 1999 Ryder Cup matches, Justin Leonard sank a crucial putt on the 17th hole of his match with Jose Marie Olazabal that virtually assured America would retain the cup. When the European press witnessed the invasion of American players' wives and girlfriends streaming onto the green in celebration, they wondered, "How is it possible they all married the same cocktail waitress."[35] The press speculated about how marriage would affect Tiger's dedication to the game. Even Jack Nicklaus questioned whether Tiger would be able to maintain his unwavering concentration when he was also responsible as a husband and father. The relationship with Jagoda lasted for two years.

In 2004 Tiger married Swedish model Elin Nordegren in a guarded ceremony in a Caribbean resort. The couple met two years earlier when she was serving as nanny for golfer Jesper Parnevik's children. As with any aspect of Tiger's personal life, the press had a voracious appetite for details, and Tiger and his representatives were just as diligent in trying to maintain his privacy. The lavish wedding took place in an exclusive resort in Barbados, and reportedly cost $2 million, and the 150 person guest list included celebrities such as Michael Jordan, Oprah Winfrey, and Bill Gates. A small army of security personnel were enlisted to provide security for the guests who were ushered onto a $57 million yacht. By this time, Team Tiger had become much more comfortable working with the media.

Earlier in Tiger's career, there were a series of incidents that could only be called public relations disasters. The first involved an award that was to honor his amateur play, and occurred as Tiger was scheduled to play in the 1996 Buick Challenge tournament. Following his unprecedented third U.S. Amateur victory in August, Tiger had played in four consecutive tournaments as a professional and had climbed to 128 on the money list, virtually assuring his place on the 1997 PGA Tour. He was exhausted and decided not to accept the sponsor's exemption for the Buick Challenge. However, he had committed to attend the Fred Haskins Award Dinner on the Thursday night during the tournament to be honored as the College Player of the Year. Given the tremendous interest Tiger had generated in his first days as a professional, the dinner was immediately sold out in anticipation of his presence.[36] When the news of his withdrawal from the tournament leaked out there was obvious disappointment, and when it was learned that he had declined to attend, the dinner was cancelled. The press savaged Tiger and his team.[37]

Immediately Tiger realized that he had made a mistake. Two weeks later he was scheduled to compete in the Las Vegas Open. He sent a letter of apology to each person who was to attend the dinner. In a column he wrote for *Golf World*, he said:

> I am human...and I do make mistakes. The decision to miss the Fred Haskins Award Dinner being held in my honor two weeks ago was one of them. Wow, did I get blasted for that and withdrawing from the Buick Challenge...I didn't realize how tired I was after the U.S. Amateur...I never got a chance to rest. I kept playing...I didn't even think about the dinner. I realize now that what I did was wrong. But hindsight is 20/20.[38]

The following year on tour there were other decisions that resulted in bad press. After winning the Masters in May, Tiger was invited to participate in a ceremony scheduled to honor the 50th anniversary of Jackie Robinson's breaking of the color line in baseball. President Clinton was to participate in the event at Shea Stadium. The invitation went through IMG and Tiger said no. Even before the fallout from this snub of the president had subsided, another controversy erupted.

There is a tradition at the Masters that the defending champion hosts the Champions Dinner, and chooses the menu on the eve of the tournament. That meant Tiger would select the menu for the 1998 dinner. During an interview with CNN, 1979 Masters Champion and tour kibitzer Fuzzy Zoeller made an offhand remark that immediately was picked up by every news organization. Concluding his complimentary remarks about Tiger's record-setting performance at the Masters, Zoeller added, "The little boy's playing great out there. Just tell him not to serve fried chicken at the [Champions] dinner next year," but then added, "Or collard greens or whatever it is they serve."[39] As a result of the comments, Zoeller took a terrible beating in the press, culminating in K-Mart, his corporate sponsor, dropping him as their spokesman. He was unable to talk to Tiger directly to apologize, and finally publicly asked Tiger to call him to discuss the incident. Several players represented by Nike called and implored Tiger to make some kind of comment to defuse the situation. It wasn't until three days after the second apology that Tiger finally made a public statement accepting Zoeller's apology. The incident did little to endear Tiger to a number of his fellow tour professionals.

Another misunderstanding further strained Tiger's relationship with his golfing colleagues. Several weeks after the Masters, Tiger was scheduled to play in the Byron Nelson Classic in Dallas. Billy Andrade was an outgoing golfer who had befriended Tiger when he first came on the tour. Andrade and Brad Faxon run a charity golf tournament in Delaware every year and as a fundraiser they ask fellow pros to sign golf balls to be auctioned. They wanted to assemble a dozen balls each signed by a Masters Champion, so they asked Tiger to provide them with a signed ball. Tiger refused. Jack Nicklaus had signed and Arnold Palmer had signed. Nick Faldo and Tom Watson had signed. When two young boys read about the story, they donated a ball Tiger had signed when he was an amateur. The actor Joe Pesci bid $50,000 for the dozen balls and gave the Tiger-autographed ball back to the two boys; the publicity about the incident resulted in a record auction for charity. Eventually Tiger donated a signed lithograph, but once again Tiger exhibited poor judgment, not atypical of a 20-year-old.[40] But Tiger was not a typical 20-year-old.

His youth also led to another problem when, according to an Associated Press report, Tiger was able to get into the Lucky Lady River Boat Casino in Iowa, using fake I.D. When the bouncer was informed that this was Tiger Woods, he was quoted as saying, "I don't care if it's the Lion King."[41]

An article in the March 1997 issue of *Gentleman's Quarterly* provided another lesson in Tiger's education in dealing with the media. Writer Charlie Pierce accompanied Tiger on a photo shoot that would appear in the magazine. Under the assumption that he was speaking off-the-record, Tiger let his guard down and told several slightly off-color jokes with racial and gay-bashing themes. The reaction to the GQ story varied. Some felt it humanized Tiger, while others felt it was just reward for limiting his interviews to a select few reporters who tended to sanitize their subject for public consumption.[42]

Despite the occasional bad press, Tiger's public image did not suffer. As he matured and began to take on more responsibility for his actions, he relied less on handlers. The result was generally better press. But famous athletes always maintain a love/hate relationship with the reporters who cover them. The reporters need access to the athletes, and so they are necessarily reluctant to criticize these people who can make or break their careers. A reporter who writes negative stories about an athlete generally loses access to that athlete. Generally the negative stories come from reporters who have been denied access to that athlete. That has been the case with Tiger.

Despite his unprecedented accomplishments on the golf course, when *Sports Illustrated* made Tiger the Sportsman of the Year 1998, Mike Lupica (*Daily News*) was quoted as saying "It's the first time they've given someone 'Sportsman of the Year' on spec."[43] In the cover story, Earl couldn't restrain himself from expressing his understandably inflated predictions for his son. He claimed that Tiger would eventually have a greater impact on society than Nelson Mandela, Gandhi, and Buddha. His reasoning was that because of modern means of communication Tiger would have a larger forum. While his reasoning was sound, it was not the sort of thing that one should actually say out loud. The reaction of the press pretty much reflected the access the respective reporters had to the Woods camp: the closer you were to the team, the less likely you were to pan Earl's comments.

But such comments only put more pressure on Tiger in his dealings with the press. It was only natural that the press expected him, as a minority, to weigh in on issues beyond the world of golf.

The most uncomfortable situation occurred during the 2003 Masters tournament. Several months before the event, Martha Burk, the president of the NOW, wrote the president of Augusta National demanding that the all-male club admit a woman member. In the months leading up to the tournament the story made front page news, culminating with the *New York Times* recommending in an editorial that Augusta should admit women and suggesting that Tiger Woods should boycott the tournament.[44] As defending champion, it was inevitable that Tiger Woods would be drawn into the controversy. Pulitzer Prize-winning columnist Dave Anderson's column encouraging Woods to play was initially suppressed by the *Times* editors. Burk called for a boycott of the tournament and urged CBS to cancel the telecast. Burk also called for Tiger to refuse to compete in protest. Opinions in the media were split. Everyone wanted a statement from Tiger. He finally spoke out on the issue, saying that he felt Augusta should allow female members, but that as a private club they should be able to deal with membership policies themselves. Not surprisingly, nobody was interested in the opinions of other golfers competing in the Masters.

It became apparent that Tiger Woods would be expected to do more than play golf. Other black athletes had established reputations for speaking out on racial issues. Jackie Robinson, Arthur Ashe, and Muhammad Ali were no strangers to controversy and spoke out on issues of race, the Vietnam War and discrimination. The press wanted Tiger to follow in that tradition; Tiger just wanted to play golf. However, the 24-hours-a-day/7-days-a-week saturation of media makes it increasingly difficult for a public person, regardless of his sphere of influence, to remain silent.

Despite his reluctance to insert himself in every political or social issue demanded by the press, Tiger, with strong support from his parents, has been committed to helping less fortunate people beyond the world of golf. Even before Tiger was making an income from playing golf, he was giving back. As a junior golfer he was offering clinics for young people, particularly minority kids. After completing his second round in the 1995 Masters, Tiger left Augusta immediately and traveled across town to the Forest Hills Golf Club, a municipal course. He conducted a clinic for a group of black children and some of the black caddies from Augusta National. Following the Masters, Tiger sent a letter to the Augusta officials thanking them for inviting him to play in the Masters. Several of the more cynical reporters dismissed his letter and the fact that he did the clinic as propaganda engineered by Earl. While questioning the motivation for Tiger's actions one writer for the *San Francisco Chronicle* made a point that had eluded other reporters: "The letter and the clinic smack ominously of a father instilling values in his son. Almost 900 golfers have played in 59 Masters tournaments, and only one of them has taken the time to give a clinic at that frumpy muni course."[45]

Whether calculated or not, immediately upon Tiger's turning professional in 1996, Tiger and Earl established the Tiger Woods Foundation. The foundation has grown in direct proportion to Tiger's accomplishments. Virtually every one of the corporations Tiger represents has some program that is connected to his foundation. His association with Target Corporation has been the most visible example of these philanthropic relationships. In addition to sponsoring a golf tournament, the Target World Challenge, the corporation has created a program designed to help young people, called "Start Something." Unlike many charity tournaments, this one gets network coverage because Tiger Woods competes in it, along with a host of other prominent pros. Recently the Woods Foundation was awarded a grant from Orange County in Southern California to build the Tiger Woods Learning Center. The Center will be an educational resource to young people of diverse backgrounds, aimed at improving reading, math and science skills. Tiger Woods is not the first wealthy person to establish a foundation with the purpose of helping kids.[46] But the level of overall positive media attention he garners assures the vital connections to the corporations that make the capital available.

In comparison to any famous professional athlete in the past, Tiger Woods is still a few years away from the prime of his career, and based on his current success in professional golf, he may be destined for other accomplishments beyond the world of sports. He began as a child prodigy, and the problem with prodigies is that they don't always fulfill the public's elevated expectations. And the public's expectations are being fanned by an evermore incendiary media. During his junior and amateur career Tiger was promoted by the media as both a model golfer and a model young man. But where he was once able to concentrate his entire being on the perfection of his golf game, he now faces the challenges of balancing the rest of his adult life with the game he plays. He is a businessman, a husband, a son, and a role model. He is a man with an exceptional ability to play the game of golf, but the media has created a situation in which he has to live up to some imaginary standard, ironically one he established—not only in golf, but also in his personal life.

After his brilliant and unprecedented introduction to professional golf in 1997, Tiger decided to completely rework his golf swing in 1998 and 1999, and though he won a major championship and nine tournaments overall, the media began to ask the question: was Tiger in a slump? The answer in 2000 was the first three legs of his Grand Slam, completed at the 2001 Masters. He went on to win Masters and U.S. Open Championships in 2002. Since then he has not won a major championship and the press again began to wonder if Tiger had lost his desire to compete. Speculation became more intense as he became more involved in outside corporate projects, devoted more time to the foundation, and became engaged and subsequently married. Then during the 2004 season Tiger did not win a stroke play tournament[47] and finished no higher than ninth in any of the majors. However, he extended his streak of consecutive cuts[48] made, a PGA Tour record, and continued to work on his game. In early 2005 he won twice and gave every indication of a new dedication to his game. The in April he won his fourth Master championship, finished second in the U.S. Open, won the British Open for a second time at St. Andrews, and finished tied for fourth in the PGA Championship. But the media and the public, as reflected by the press, wants perfection.

It is impossible to examine the life of Tiger Woods without observing the growing and inexhaustible need the public has for more personal information about interesting, accomplished, and beautiful people. Media executives argue that it is the public that creates the need and that the media simply satisfies the need, but that's an oversimplification. The question should be: How accurate is the information the media is dispensing? With the ever-growing number of media outlets there is an increasing need for more information to fill the increased time and space, but there is less and less time for reflection. Print journalism was always controlled by a deadline, but the electronic media have virtually eliminated the chance to check facts. Because of the printing process there was some opportunity for editors to review copy, check facts, and verify sources. With instantaneous modern media distribution, the practice of editing before distributing information on a media outlet is a luxury that competition renders obsolete. It is becoming more difficult for even the most concerned, careful, and conscientious reporter to take a sufficient amount of time to complete even rudimentary research. There was a time when the book was the most reliable source of information. It was a cumbersome process and cost a great deal of money to write, print, and distribute, but these very factors assured an element of veracity. Today the Internet makes it possible to get access to millions of sources without leaving your study. And while conducting research on the Internet, in and of itself is not bad, it does pose the danger of relying on information that may be of questionable origins. Ultimately the most reliable sources for reporters are the people they cover. But the closer reporters get to the source, the less objective they become.

Tiger Woods is a good example of this catch-22. John Feinstein, an excellent writer and commentator, has been the most critical of Tiger, and more particularly the influence IMG exerted on him early in his career. Feinstein, presumably because of his negative articles, has had little access to Team Tiger. Reporters who have good things to say about Tiger and Earl tend to be allowed to get closer to Tiger and his team. Those that don't, aren't. If reporters are denied access to the source, than what we know comes either directly from the source or a reporter who is close to the source. Most of what the public knows about Earl, for example, comes from his own books.

Earl Woods is clearly a man who feels he has done a good job raising his son and wants some credit. But he has alluded to the fact that no matter how good a parent he might have been, Tiger's development as a person and as a golfer is driven by something beyond his parents. Earl made the mistake of saying that very thing out loud, and the press jumped on him. He has talked candidly about his first marriage publicly, and the problems with his former wife after Tiger became successful. He does still have a decent relationship with his kids from his first marriage, and he does admit he was not a very good father to them. He has even been quite forthcoming about the current relationship with Kultida. So it's hard to accuse him of trying to sugarcoat his life. It's difficult to take to task the man who raised Tiger Woods.

The question then becomes: can we not just appreciate excellence for what it is? Does Tiger Woods have to do anything other than excel at golf? Does he also have to speak for all people who have been or ever will be discriminated against? Is it not enough that he has succeeded as a minority in the professional sport that most epitomizes privilege and exclusion? Most professional golfers on the PGA Tour went to college on golf scholarships and when they graduated went directly into a job that afforded luxuries not normally associated with the masses. They operate as independent contractors or entrepreneurs, and they tend to be conservative in their politics. Tiger Woods is the closest thing to diversity in the upper echelons of touring golf professionals.

Tiger Woods continues to be measured by a different yardstick than other golfers on the PGA Tour. Most professional athletes scoff at the idea that they have a responsibility as role models. Tiger Woods has the opportunity to become the greatest golfer ever, and along the way provide a role model for young people, especially minorities. By any account, so far he's done a pretty good job.

NOTES

1. John R. Catsis, *Sports Broadcasting* (Chicago: Nelson-Hall Publishers 1996), 5.

2. Ibid., 16.

3. Ibid., 27.

4. Ibid., 32.

5. This cut down significantly on production costs since the broadcasters didn't have to travel and their headquarters were in New York.

6. Ibid., 30.

7. Ibid., 16.

8. Ibid., 93.

9. The Masters, "Official Site of the Masters Tournament," http://www.masters.org/en_US/history/jacket/palmer.html.

10. The Masters, "Official Site of the Masters Tournament," http://www.masters.org/en_US/history/jacket/palmer.html.

11. Louisville Slugger Museum, http://www.slugger.com/museum/

12. Curt Sampson, *Chasing Tiger* (Atria Books, 2002), 195.

13. John Feinstein, *The First Coming,* (New York: Ballantine, 1998), 17.

14. As quoted in Sampson ,196.

15. Michael Sokolove, "Constructing a Teen Phenom," *New York Times Magazine*, 22 November 22 2004, 81.

16. Sampson, 208.

17. Feinstein, 58–59.

18. As quoted in Tom Callahan, *In Search of Tiger* (New York: Crown Publisher, 2003), 142.

19. As quoted in Tim Rosaforte, *Tiger Woods: The Making of A Champion* (New York: St. Martin's Press, 1997), 142.

20. John Strege, *A Biography of Tiger Woods* (New York: Broadway Books, 1998), 195.

21. David Owen, *The Chosen One* (New York: Simon & Schuster, 2001), 35.

22. Sampson, 205.

23. Titleist Company, "Titleist," http://www.titleist.com/mediacenter/press releases.asp.

24. Strege, 189.

25. Owen, 206.

26. Sampson, 212.

27. Ibid., 210.

28. Rosaforte, 179.

29. Earl Woods, *Playing Through* (New York: HarperCollins, 1998), 185.

30. Rosaforte, 55.

31. As quoted in ibid., 182–183.

32. The author was also involved with the National Minority Golf Foundation, served on a committee with Earl Woods, and had an opportunity to play a round of golf with him at Doral.

33. L. Price, "Tunnel Vision," *Sports Illustrated*, 3 April 2000, 56.

34. As quoted in Rosaforte, 185.

35. As quoted in Callahan, 205.

36. The problem was exacerbated when Hughes Norton read a statement by Tiger, rather then Tiger making the statement in person.

37. Rosaforte, 76.

38. As quoted in Strege, 205.

39. As quoted in Feinstein, 64.

40. Ibid., 71.

41. As quoted in Rosaforte, 81.

42. Charles Pierce, "The Man, Amen," *Chasing Tiger*, ed. Glenn Stout (Cambridge: Da Capo Press, 2002), 93.

43. As quoted in Rosaforte, 114.

44. Richard Baehr, "Thank You Martha," *American Thinker*, 14 April 2004 http://www.americanthinker.com.

45. As quoted in Strege, 108.

46. Tiger Woods Foundation, http://twfound.org.

47. He won the WGC Accenture Match Play tournament.

48. Most PGA tournaments (and the U.S. Open and Masters) make cuts of the players with scores above a predetermined line, usually after the second round of competitions.

BIBLIOGRAPHY

BOOKS

Andrisani, John. *Think Like A Tiger: An Analysis of Tiger Woods' Mental Game.* New York: Berkley Publishing Group, 2002.

Anselmo, John. *"A-Game" Golf: The Complete Starter Kit for Golfers.* New York: Random House, 2001.

Ashe, Arthur Jr. *A Hard Road to Glory: 1919 to 1945.* New York: Warner Books, 1988.

Callahan, Tom. *In Search of Tiger: A Journey Through Golf with Tiger Woods.* New York: Crown Publishing Group, 2003.

Catsis, John R. *Sports Broadcasting.* Chicago: Nelson Hall Publishers, 1996.

Concannon, Dale. *Golf, the Early Days: Royal & Ancient Game from Its Origins to 1939.* London: Salamander Books, 1995.

Crosby, Don. *"Tiger Woods Made Me Look Like a Genius."* Kansas City, Kans.: Andrew McMeel Publishing, 2000.

Duran, Rudy. *In Every Kid There Lurks a Tiger.* New York: Hyperion, 2002.

Edwards, Nicholas. *Tiger Woods: An American Master.* New York: Scholastic Inc., 1997.

Feinstein, John. *A Good Walk Spoiled: Days and Nights on the PGA Tour.* Boston: Little, Brown and Co., 1995.

———. *Open: Inside the Ropes at Bethpage Black.* Boston: Little, Brown and Co., 2003.

———. *The First Coming, Tiger Woods: Master or Martyr?* New York: Ballantine Publishing Group, 1998.

———. *The Majors.* Boston: Little, Brown and Co., 1999.

Frost, Mark. *The Grand Slam: Bobby Jones, America, and the Story of Golf*. New York: Hyperion, 2004.

————. *The Greatest Game Ever Played: Harry Vardon, Francis Ouimet, and the Birth of Modern Golf*. New York: Hyperion, 2002.

"Golf." *The World Book Encyclopedia*. Chicago: Field Enterprises Educational Corporation, 1976, 255.

Gutman, Bill. *Tiger Woods: A Biography*. New York: Pocket Books, 1997.

McCormack, Mark H. *What They Don't Teach You at Harvard Business School: Notes From Street-Smart Executive*. New York: Bantam Books, 1984.

McDaniel, Pete. *Uneven Lies: The Heroic Story of African-Americans in Golf*. Greenwich, Conn.: The American Golfer, 2000.

Owen, David. *The Chosen One: Tiger Woods and the Dilemma of Greatness*. New York: Simon & Schuster, 2001.

Roberts, Jeremy. *Tiger Woods*. Minneapolis, Minn.: Lerner Publsihing Group, 2002.

Robinson, Jr., Lenwood. *Skins & Grins: The Plight of the Black American Golfer*. Evanston, Ill.: Chicago Spectrum Press, 1997.

Rosaforte, Tim. *Raising the Bar: The Championship Years of Tiger Woods*. New York: Thomas Dunne Books, 2000

————. *Tiger Woods: The Making of a Champion*. New York: St. Martin's Press, 1997.

Sampson, Curt. *Chasing Tiger*. New York: Atria Books, 2002.

Schultz, Brad. *Sports Broadcasting*. Boston: Focal Press, 2002.

Sluby, Sr., Paul E. *The Family Recollections of Beulah A. Shippen and Mabel S.(Shippen) Hatcher*, (Self-published, 1994), 43.

Stout, Glenn, ed. *Chasing Tiger: The Tiger Woods Reader*. Cambridge: Da Capo Press, 2002.

Sifford, Charlie. *"Just Let Me Play": The Story of Charlie Sifford, The First Black PGA Golfer*. Lathan, New York: British American Publishing, 1992.

Sinnette, Calvin. *Forbidden Fairways: African Americans and the Game of Golf*. Chelsea, Minn: Sleeping Bear Press, 1998.

Stafford, Ian. *In Search of the Tiger*. New York: Random House, 2003.

Strege, John. *A Biography of Tiger Woods*. New York: Broadway Books, 1997.

Williams, Michael. *The History of Golf*. Secaucus, N.J.: Cartwell Books, 1985.

Woods, Earl. *Playing Through: Straight Talk on Hard Work, Big Dreams and Adventures with Tiger Woods*. New York: HarperCollins, 1998.

————. *Training A Tiger: A Father's Guide to Raising a Winner Both in Golf and in Life*. New York: HarperCollins, 1997.

Young, A.S. *Negro First in Sports*. Chicago: Johnson Publishing Co., 1963.

MAGAZINES

Golf Digest, November 1980, 15.

The Golfer, 5 August 1896, 109.

"In the Crowd," *Sports Illustrated,* 24 September 1990.

Jones, Guilford. "Past Greats." *Black Sports,* July 1973, 65–66.

Londino, Lawrence. "Shady Rest: Itself a Strong Ship." *Golf Journal,* spring 1996, 17.

Lux, Ron. "Golf Pioneers by Necessity." *Golf Leisure,* fall 1989, 32.

Price, L. "Tunnel Vision." *Sports Illustrated,* 3 April 2000, 56.

Sokolove, Michael. "Constructing A Teen Phenom." *New York Times Magazine,* 28 November 2004, 80.

Strafaci, Frank. "Forgotten Pioneer Professional." *Golfing Magazine,* March 1957, 11.

VIDEO

Golf Talk Live. The Golf Channel, 18 December 1996.

A Place For Us: The Story of Shady Rest and America's First Golf Professional. Directed by Larry Londino, WNET Channel 13, New York, 19 December 1996.

Tiger Woods: Son, Hero & Champion. Trans World International, 1997.

The Tiger Woods Story. Directed by LeVar Burton. Paramount Pictures, 1998.

Tiger Woods: The Authorized DVD Collection. Golf Channel Documentary, February 2005.

INTERNET

Atlanta History Center. "Down the Fairway with Bobby Jones." http://www.bobbyjonesgolfexhibit.com/Timeline/main_timeline.html.

Baehr, Richard. "Thank You Martha." *American Thinker,* 14 April 2004, http://www.americanthinker.com.

"Big 12 Conference." http://www.britannica.com/eb/article?tocId=9079156.

Chadchaidee, Thanapol. *Buddhism in Thailand.* 28 December 2004, http://sunsite.au.ac.th/thailand/buddhism/.

"History of Special Forces, 1961–1971." Department of Army Publication. 1989. http://www.specialoperations.com/Army/Special_Forces/default.html.

Louisville Slugger Museum. www.sluggermuseum.com.

The Masters. "Official Site of the Masters Tournament." http://www.masters.org/en_US/history/jacket/palmer.html.

PGA Tour. "Notah Begay-Media Guide." http://www.pgatour.com/players/bio/149683.

Titleist Company. "Titleist." http://www.titleist.com/mediacenter/pressreleases.asp.

Tiger Woods. "Official Website for Tiger Woods." http://www.tigerwoods.com.

United States Golf Association. "USGA History." http://www.usga.org/aboutus/usga_history/usga_history.html.

U.S. Department of Justice. "Faces of the ADA—Casey Martin continues his professional golf career." 17 July 2000. http://www.usdoj.gov/crt/ada/fmartin.htm.

NEWSPAPERS

Baltimore Afro-American, 18 July 1925: 6.

Cataclysm, Social. "Only Golf Course in U.S. Is Thriving in Suburban Jersey," *New York Sun*, 11 July 1922: 22.

Drape, Joe. "New Study Shows Gap on Court and in Class." *New York Times*, 16 March 2005: D5.

"Elder Denies He Made Charge of Race Bias in Pensacola Golf," *New York Times*, 6 June 1969: 49.

Izenberg, Jerry. *Sunday Star Ledger* [Newark], 17 June 1984: 28.

Mardo, Bill. "2 Negros Golfers Sue PGA for $250,000," *Daily Worker*, 16 January 1948: Back page.

"Masters Policy Change Seen As Aid to Blacks," *New York Times*, 13 June 1971: Sec. V, 5.

"P.G.A. Committee Votes to Ease Tourney Ban on Negro Players," *New York Times*, 14 January 1952: 25.

"P.G.A. Will Shift '62 Tourney Site," *New York Times*, 18 May 1961: 45.

"Thousands Motored Out to Shady Rest Country Club Decoration Day," *Amsterdam News* [New York], 6 June 1923: 5.

Walton, Lester A. "Shady Rest Club Ends Big Fight in Jersey Courts," *Pittsburgh Courier*, 18 July 1925: 9.

Werden, Lincoln A. "4 Men Removed After Heckling Sifford, Negro Golf Pro, in Greensboro Open," *New York Times*, 5 April 1969: 35.

Werden, Lincoln A. "18 in House Demand Masters Invite Black Golfer," *New York Times*, 18 March 1973: 1.

Werden, Lincoln A. "Special-Bid Idea Disliked by Elder,"*New York Times*, 20 March 1973: 45.

"Will Not Bar Negroes: P.G.A. Revises Attitude, Suit by 3 Pros Dismissed," *New York Times*, 22 September 1948: 45.

"Will Not Bar Negroes," *New York Times*, 23 November 1960: 163

OTHER

Preiss, Richard Porter. "Mashies At Mapledale: A Black Country Club in Massachusetts During the 1920s." Paper presented at North American Society for Sport History Convention, Vancouver, British Columbia, Canada, 24–25 May 1986: 1.

INDEX

About the Author

LAWRENCE J. LONDINO is chair of the Department of Broadcasting at Montclair State University. He has written, produced and directed a variety of radio, television and film projects over a 30-year career, most recently a public television documentary, *A Place For Us: The Story of Shady Rest and America's First Golf Professional*, which traced the history of African-Americans playing golf in New Jersey.